THE DIFFERENCE IN BEING
A CHRISTIAN TODAY

Books by JOHN A. T. ROBINSON
Published by THE WESTMINSTER PRESS

The Difference in Being a Christian Today
Christian Freedom in a Permissive Society
The New Reformation?
Christian Morals Today
Liturgy Coming to Life
Honest to God
On Being the Church in the World

The Difference in Being a Christian Today

by JOHN A. T. ROBINSON

THE WESTMINSTER PRESS
Philadelphia

ACKNOWLEDGEMENTS

The author and publishers would like to acknowledge their indebtedness for permission to reproduce copyright material as follows: from the New English Bible, New Testament, 2nd edition © 1970 by permission of Oxford and Cambridge University Presses; from *For the Time Being* by W. H. Auden, published by Faber & Faber, London, 1945; from 'Dichotomy Then Integration' by Helder Camara, published in *New Christian*, 14 May 1970; from *Songs of Sydney Carter: In the Present Tense*, Book 2 © 1969 Galliard Ltd.; from *Ministry in Question* edited by A. Gilmore, published by Darton, Longman & Todd, London, 1971; from 'Old Tom's Scruples' by Thomas Kretz, published in *The Christian Century*, 12 November 1969, copyright 1969 Christian Century Foundation, reprinted by permission; from 'The Pope and the Archbishop' by Peter Lewis, published in the *Daily Mail*, 5 December 1970; from *Beyond the Stable State* by Donald Schon, published by Maurice Temple-Smith, December 1970; from *The Hospital—A Place of Truth* by Michael Wilson, published by the Institute for the Study of Worship and Religious Architecture, University of Birmingham, 1971.

CONTENTS

PREFACE

The first four chapters of this book originally formed the substance of a course of University Sermons at Great St Mary's, Cambridge, in the Lent Term 1971. They were then expanded and increased in number for delivery as the Carnahan Lectures at the Union Theological Seminary, Buenos Aires, in July 1971. They have subsequently been further revised and enlarged in the light of the questions and discussion. I am profoundly indebted to the invitation and the stimulus of both these centres. The contrast, and the complementarity, of the old world and the third world are essential factors in any appreciation of the difference in being a Christian today.

As this book goes through the press, I have learnt of the death at a tragically early age of Professor John Litwiller, Rector of the Seminary in Buenos Aires, who with his wife looked after us so graciously. His leadership will be sorely missed, and I should like to dedicate this book to his memory.

JOHN ROBINSON
October 1971

ONE

THE END OF THE
STABLE STATE

'The difference in being a Christian today': there is in the title a deliberate ambiguity—depending on whether you stress the difference in being a *Christian* today (rather than, say, a humanist) or whether you stress the difference in being a Christian *today* (rather than yesterday). And the answer to each is closely connected with the answer to the other—as can be seen if I put it another way.

The contemporary Christian, unless totally closed to the winds that blow, finds himself (both as an individual and as a Church member) caught up in an identity crisis. Just who is he? Where does he stand? What does he stand for? And an identity crisis has this same double aspect. The dictionary defines 'identity' as 'individuality' and 'absolute sameness'. Individuality: 'Who am I in relation to those around me? What is my distinctive role?' And sameness: 'Who am I in relation to my past? Am I the person that I was?' If we cannot answer either or both, we become uncertain of ourselves, and a crisis of confidence results. The most reassuring assumption is that the answer to each is the same—that we maintain our identity in the sense of our distinctive role by maintaining absolute sameness.

And this applies still more powerfully to institutions. The persona of Trinity College, Cambridge, is effortlessly asserted by the words that look down on us from the royal motto above High Table: *semper eadem*— always the same. Similarly in the Church, the test of catholicity, the criterion of what is quintessentially Christian, has been the so-called Vincentian Canon: *'quod ubique, quod semper, quod ab omnibus creditum est'*—what has been believed everywhere, always and by everyone.

But this has given the Church (like other long-established institutions) a vested interest in stability, and a corresponding fear of change as a double threat to its identity. For if it is not the same as what it was, what is it at all? Confronted with what Donald Schon, the American business psychologist, in his BBC Reith Lectures, *Change and Industrial Society*, called 'the loss of the stable state', there is a condition of 'uncertainty'. And by uncertainty, he said, he did not mean risk, 'which is a probability ratio which we all know how to handle', but something more unnerving. He described it vividly like this:

> If I arrive on a desert island and it's dark, and I don't know the place and I see a girl standing there who seems rather suspicious to me, and someone sitting opposite me, and I think there's a bulge in his pocket, and he has a queen and an ace and I have two aces, and I hear a strange noise and the lights dim, then I'm in a situation of uncertainty.[1]

Maybe it's difficult to recognize quite such an intriguing or dramatic situation in the Church. Indeed, I would want to qualify his metaphor 'the loss of the stable state' and point out that it cannot simply be applied to persons and to institutions composed of persons. It is taken from physics, from the world of inorganic matter. When a critical mass or a critical temperature is reached, an explosion takes place or a liquid turns into a gas. And this is a sudden transition in which the second state simply cancels and replaces the first. But this is not true of the organic world. An organism maintains its identity precisely through change—if it doesn't change, it dies— and the process of metabolism is constant and continuous. And this is true even when the change of degree is so great as to constitute to all appearances a change of kind—for instance, when a caterpillar changes into a chrysalis and a chrysalis into a butterfly. There is anything but 'absolute sameness', yet it is this butterfly that was this chrysalis that was this caterpillar, and not another.

All metaphors are dangerous if pressed, and even organic ones cannot simply be transferred to persons, if only because while we are being changed we can reflect on the change as it were from outside it. Nevertheless I have called this introductory chapter 'The End of the Stable State'. For I agree with Schon in thinking that spiritually, as in other ways, we are faced with the *sort* of critical change that can be likened to what happens when the laws governing solids or liquids give place to the laws governing gases. When qualifications are necessary we can make them, but at least the metaphor has the merit of alerting us to the fact that something may be happening to which the traditional responses, however attuned to change, are not going to be adequate.

Indeed, I believe the crucial divide in the Church today—cutting across all denominations and parties and even, as I know from myself, individuals—is between those who basically accept (and even welcome) the end of the stable state (however painful) and those who deny or resist it. This is what distinguishes the radical and conservative responses (and there is a mixture of both in most of us). The difference, I would stress, is *not*—and God forbid that either side should say or imply it—that one group is more or less Christian than the other. It is simply that they honestly differ in assessing what is happening. One believes that the same model, whether of truth or morality, spirituality or structure, can basically go on; the other that, if we are really to understand the change we are in and respond to it creatively, we have got to be open to a fundamentally new model. Let me explain.

The stable state has been characterized by what Donald Schon called the centre-periphery model. He was talking primarily about business and government, but exactly the same has been true of education and culture and the Church. Indeed, he cited the Jesuits, along with Coca Cola, as a classic instance of its simplicity and efficiency.

Within the Church as a whole the supreme example has of course been the structure of Roman Catholicism. But in Church history any denomination, when it makes the break of setting up on its own and achieving its own identity, has tended to become a little catholicism. A good instance of this is the transition in early Methodism from being a society (of methodical Anglicans) to becoming a Church. And structurally the Methodist Church—with its annual conference responsible finally for all decisions, working down through districts and circuits—is probably today the most centralized of the lot. I once asked Dr Newton Flew, the then Principal of Wesley House, Cambridge, what was the distinctive contribution of Methodism (its 'identity'), and he replied without hesitation, 'The best discipline outside Rome'. In the present state of the Roman Communion (and I never meet a Roman Catholic who believes in the Pope as he expects to be believed in, any more than I ever meet an American who believes in the War!) Methodism may even have moved to the top of that league.

Anyhow, the model, in whatever disrepair in all our traditions, is one that we readily recognize. It rests upon a firm centre—though, with expansion, you will soon have sub-centres—disseminating outwards towards the periphery in the furthest mission station. And it applies not only to organization but to ideas and life-style. The whole identity-structure of Christianity, which enables you to 'know where you are', whether in faith or morals or church services, has presupposed the same model of a centre linked radially and authoritatively with a circumference.

Moreover, it has been a peculiar feature of the Christian Church (and particularly of the Christian west) that it has been as much concerned with edges as with centres.

In business or colonial government or education the edges of your empire or influence shade off: it is difficult, and unimportant, to draw lines. But the Christian Church, much more than other religions, has been a great line-drawer. It has been heavily preoccupied with definitions, with heresies and schisms, tests and anathemas. And when you operate with the belief that outside the Church there is no salvation or with excommunication as the ultimate sanction (even, believe it or not, at one stage in the Byzantine Church for playing chess), it becomes rather vital to say just who, or what, is 'in' rather than 'out'.

Creeds, codes, cults have all served as what the Thirty-nine Articles of the Church of England call a 'mark of difference, whereby Christian men are discerned from others that be not'. According to this model, the distinctive has been defined in terms of the exclusive, and the centre in terms of uniformity (even, theoretically, in Anglicanism, the most fuzzy example of such a constitution). Its great asset was that it gave you a *locus standi*, so that you could sum up what it means to be a Christian by pointing—for instance with the Church Catechism—to such clearly defined foci as the Creed, the Lord's Prayer and the Ten Commandments.

Now all that, it appears, seems to have gone. We are constantly told that on faith, on morals, on private prayer, public worship, church discipline, or the meaning of mission, people 'just don't know where they are'. They complain of being hopelessly confused, of everything being so vague. And I am aware of being regarded as a prime confuser. Even as I prepared this, an article appeared in the *Daily Mail* to whose interesting conclusion I shall return. But it took off from the position that 'ever since Bishop Robinson published *Honest to God* the Church of England has been a mass of long-buried doubts, and it would be hard to find a consensus of opinion of what its doctrine is'.[2] I cannot lay claim to such single-handed desolation. But I recognize the state of uncertainty, and that is why I have chosen this theme. For people are genuinely bewildered (though others are correspondingly liberated). They feel they have lost their bearings—and that in the one area of life which they trusted would remain an island of security in a sea of change. For religion told you what to believe, what to do and what to expect. But with even that dissolving there is anxiety and not a little resentment—and a hankering after fixed points, however few. 'Will the Bishop of Woolwich tell us what articles of the Creed he does believe?' ran a letter in *The Times* from a peer—as if it were all a reductionist exercise, the same model but on a smaller scale.

Let me say at once that I have very genuine sympathy, especially with the older generation. Indeed it is often difficult not to get shaken oneself. For, as Donald Schon pointed out, previously the time required for new ideas or new inventions to become diffused was above the threshold of generational change—that is to say, it took longer than one generation for what was new at the centre to reach the periphery. Society, like nature, accommodated to change basically by individuals dying off—new methods, new men. Now the rate of change requires us to live several life-times in one.

But not only this. I suspect with him that the familiar, reassuring centre-periphery pattern is itself on the way out. Partly this is because what he called its infra-structure has changed without possibility of reverse. The old pattern of communication from centre to edges depended on the road, the railway, the trade-route, the telegraph. The new on the mass media, the jet plane, the satellite. Ideas which a hundred years ago (for instance about Adam and Eve) took several generations to be funnelled down from professor to pulpit to pew, and still have hardly reached the man in the street, today are flashed around the world in seconds. Moreover they observe no recognized chain of communication but pop up anywhere. The society of the United States is effectively being changed, as Schon well illustrated, more than by the White House or the Pentagon, by kaleidoscopic movements with constantly shifting leadership and interconnected causes relating to civil rights, peace, poverty, free speech and the like, which have no fixed centres and no clear edges.

The silent majority in Church as in State yearns wistfully—or stridently—for a return to the stable state in a new form. And in both at the moment, in Britain at any rate, the swing is to the conservatives. Indeed, as I said earlier, there will be no sudden transition: the overlap will be with us for a long time, and there will not be a simple replacement. But I would urge as strongly as I can that instead of looking only to what can be salvaged from the old identities we must ask boldly whether distinctively Christian existence is likely in future to be characterized by this 'in or out' model, by a body of doctrine, a code of behaviour, a pattern of spirituality, a religious organization, which is peculiar to Christians and marks them off by exclusion from others.

What then is the mark of our identity today? Is it 'absolute sameness' with the past? It can't be—or if it is I for one am convinced we haven't a future. Is it 'individuality' in the sense of being 'a peculiar people' separated from other men? I believe it would be truer to say that we find our identity by losing it in identification, that we are *distinctive precisely as we are not distinct*.

Such a statement obviously needs to be explained and expanded—as I seek to do in the chapters that follow. But try this for a fit. It comes from the programme prepared by the Chaplaincy to London University, for a mission to be led there by the Archbishop of Canterbury:

The Christian life is not the creation of a separate kind of existence; nor is it the creation of a separate form of religious life; nor the following of an exclusively Christian way of life. Rather, the Christian life

is the strengthening, promotion and celebration of all
good and genuine human life.[3]

For those who know it (and I shall cite it in the next
chapter) these words echo with strange familiarity a
famous passage from a Christian writing of the second
century. There is nothing new about them. But the
immediate forebear of this theology is Dietrich Bonhoeffer
who wrote from prison: 'To be a Christian does not
mean to be religious in a particular way . . . but to be
a man.'[4]

But immediately the question arises: What then is the
difference between a Christian and a humanist? This is
the central question to which I shall be coming back from
various angles. But let me say this now. In that letter
Bonhoeffer goes on—in words curiously omitted from the
first, and unfortunately most widespread, English translation: 'To be a Christian does not mean to be religious
in a particular way . . . but to be a man—not a type of
man, but *the man that Christ creates in us.*' That is to
say, the true dimension of humanness is not what we are
when left to ourselves, but what we have it in us to become when taken out of ourselves into the full potential
stature of humanity in Christ.

It all depends on what it means ultimately to be human.
For the Christian (as indeed for the Marxist) man is to
be defined in terms of what he is open to. And it is in its
estimate of this that the Christian faith differs from a
closed humanism, which makes of the *humanum* (on the
content of which we have much in common) an 'ism',
or interpretation of the whole in terms of a part. Such a
world-view is clearly incompatible with Christianity: for
man is not the measure of all things. Yet I don't want
to be put in the position of defining myself as a Christian
as *opposed* to a humanist. I am happy—with Erasmus
and many others from the Renaissance onwards—to call
myself a Christian humanist—a Christian who treasures
the humanist values, which indeed modern humanists

have largely taken from Christianity. Of course, as well as common ground there will be partings of the ways, sticking points, goings of the second mile, judgements passed —by secular humanists on Christians as well as the other way round. For their perspectives are not the same. The Christian sees what it means to be a man in Christ— and what he sees in Christ is the clue not only to human nature but to the whole *milieu divin* (as Teilhard de Chardin called it) by which man is surrounded.

All this I shall be trying to elucidate and spell out in terms of the Way, the Truth and the Life—today. But let me return now in closing to the note on which I began. Because of its double threat to their identity Christians have been extraordinarily fearful of change, as they have been extraordinarily fearful of freedom. But change, like freedom, is the very matrix of renewal, of that 'planned obsolescence' in which the gospel consists of the God who says, 'Behold! I am making all things new!' Suppose we do face an end to the stable state we have known. In such a situation, says Jesus, Christians and others should be distinguished by their responses—and it is a very real sign of difference:

Nations will stand helpless, not knowing which way to turn from the roar and surge of the sea; men will faint with terror at the thought of all that is coming upon the world.

But

When all this begins to happen, stand upright and hold your heads high, because your liberation is near.[5]

And if, as Christians, we imagine things today are exceptionally difficult, listen to another Cambridge man speaking exactly a hundred years ago, the gentle and scholarly Dr Hort, who with Westcott and Lightfoot steered the Church in England through the storms of biblical criticism in the nineteenth century. He too was speaking on 'the Way, the Truth and the Life':

If now, by a voice which cannot be disobeyed, the

Church is summoned to know as truth what it has hitherto chiefly held as sacred tradition, the prospect may seem as alarming as when the disciples learned that the Teacher's voice would soon no longer be heard among them. . . . Assuredly many a weak or hasty soul will be stricken with spiritual palsy, and many a strong soul with sadness, while the work goes on. Yet so it has been in every great crisis of the Church by which the kingdom of God has made a swift advance. If we stop to count the falling or fallen, no battle will ever be won.[6]

Or, for our brasher and less gracious age, here is a poem by an American Jesuit, Thomas Kretz, on the modern religious wilderness:

> A season of doubt
> storms ashen temples
> hollow as Roman ruins
> bleached by sun without shade,
> gutted by idle time
> quarrelling with wind,
> sharp rain pecking illusions;
> an exclusive forum
> crumbling around myopia:
>
> first the skyscraper disintegrated
> into individual stones
> of private theology,
> then limbo collapsed
> in a dusty heap of mercy;
> yesterday the wall failed
> exposing faulty structures;
> tomorrow men will control
> the number of God's images.
>
> Fear palpitates doubt
> *but*
> *love bursts blood vessels too.*[7]

I am one of those who, with fear and trembling, welcome the end of the stable state. But this does not mean that I wish wantonly to pull down or to deny the old. Yet it seems difficult not to get the name of being an iconoclast! I feel some sympathy for St Stephen, of whom they said:

This man is for ever saying things against this holy place and against the Law. For we have heard him say that Jesus of Nazareth will destroy this place and alter the customs handed down to us by Moses.[8]

Yet this charge is introduced by the words: 'They produced false witnesses who said . . .'. And the saying Stephen is supposed to have cited from Jesus is itself in the Gospels stated to rest on false witness. (Such is the way in my experience that press reports build upon each other!) Jesus did not say *he* would destroy the Temple. What he may have said is what St John reports: '*Destroy this temple, and in three days I will raise it again.*'[9] He could see that it was doomed. But the destruction would be the work of others. *His* word was not a negative one but a word of encouragement and hope. Even if one stone were not left upon another (and, as we know from present-day Jerusalem, it didn't in fact quite come to that), this would not be the end, but the beginning. That didn't mean that he did not love the Temple and value it: indeed, he wept over it and risked arrest for it to be what it was meant to be, a truly ecumenical centre, a place of prayer for all nations.'

Similarly, if I appear to some to be threatening to the structures of faith or of morals or of Church, it is not because I have any desire to knock them. I am well aware that for many, as indeed for myself, 'there is a blessing in them'. Yet they *are* under a hammering, and it is very possible (to put it no higher) that in their present form they may not survive. They can be defended, and there are those who, very properly, will want to defend them. I do not in the least question the value or the integrity of what they are doing. Indeed, I shall presuppose rather than attack that line of apologetic (which with one part of me I could happily undertake myself). But in what follows I shall deliberately be taking the other side, asking what happens if we *accept* the end of the stable state, the decay and death of the body we have known—even if in fact (as is more than probable) it doesn't quite come to that. This is not a prospect of gloom. For I believe in resurrection—even if not always in three days!

TWO

THE WAY—NOW

In his Christmas oratorio, *For the Time Being*, W. H.
Auden makes the three wise men explain what led them
to Bethlehem. The first says,

> To discover how to be truthful now
> Is the reason I follow this star.

The second says,

> To discover how to be living now
> Is the reason I follow this star.

The third says,

> To discover how to be loving now
> Is the reason I follow this star.

Then to sum up all say,

> To discover how to be human now
> Is the reason we follow this star.[1]

How to be human now: that is the greatest single
search that unites our distracted world. If the Christian
message is to have any relevance, it will be because it
comes to men as an answer to that question. This is an
indispensable mark of distinctively Christian existence today. In Bonhoeffer's words I quoted previously, 'To be
a Christian does not mean to be religious in a particular
way . . . but to be a man'—the full, free, mature human
being that Christ can make of us.

In this and the next two chapters I propose to take the
three ingredients of being human on which Auden fastens
—what it means to be truthful, living and loving now.
And, as I indicated, I should like to do this under the
same three heads that Hort chose for his famous Hulsean
Lectures in Cambridge in 1871—*The Way, the Truth, the*

Life. This involves an alteration in Auden's order of how to be truthful, living and loving. But there is a reason for it. For, as Hort put it, 'The Way lies most on the surface as presented to our faculties; further down lies the Truth, and beneath the Truth the Life.'[2]

The way is the natural point of entry, especially for this generation. For it is a pragmatic, functional age: 'Don't talk to me, show me.' And Christianity was known as 'the way' before it was known as anything else. It is primarily a style of life, a pattern of living. Moreover, this is the product it has publicly to show to the world. This represents its store-front. Behind that indeed lies a belief and at the heart of that belief an interior life. The rule of faith and the rule of prayer may logically, or ontologically, be prior. But Christians have frequently made the mistake of regarding these as what in business would be called the point of sale. I remember a woman coming to see me after *Honest to God* who said that it seemed that what the Church had to say to her was, 'Come to Evensong and stand up and say the Creed', and she commented, 'I feel I neither want to nor can'. But in early Christianity these things—the symbols of faith and worship—were the arcana, the mysteries. What was public property was the way, and it was this that had to face the test of open scrutiny.

'Let your aims', said St Paul, 'be such as all men count honourable'; or St Peter, 'Let all your behaviour be such as even pagans can recognize as good'.[3] 'Behaviour' here is what the Authorized Version translated as 'conversation', which meant not as it does now, talking, but living (even in the phrase 'the conversation of the wives'!). The Greek word means literally walking up and down in the street. It refers to how you go about your daily business, how you relate to the world. Distinctively Christian existence is therefore, as Bonhoeffer stressed, essentially something secular. It is a life-style for anyone, not for a peculiarly holy or religious group.

For it is a way of being human, not a way of living a separated existence. That is what it was about Jesus that shocked the Pharisees, whose name simply means 'the separatists': he mixed, he was common.

Hence the similarity between the way as seen by Christians and as seen by the best humanists is not, as it appears to so many churchmen, a threat, but a confirmation. They properly feel that there ought to be a difference. But to put the difference here is to put it in the wrong place. For if Christianity is the truth about what it means to be human, then our aim should be to have more rather than less in common, and we should rejoice when we find a convergence. For the truly human is not one thing for Christians and another thing for non-Christians.

Consider, for instance, such a basic human relationship as marriage. You sometimes hear people talk as though there were two different species—Christian marriage and non-Christian marriage (which quickly tend to be equated with church weddings and state weddings!). But there is no such thing as Christian marriage, any more than Christian birth or Christian parenthood. There is marriage, entered into by Christians and by non-Christians: it is a natural sacrament of which the parties themselves are the minister (even in the most churchy of weddings). And the Christian aim for marriage is the same for all men— the greatest possible fulfilment of the human potential in mutual self-giving and in the awesome responsibility of pro-creation.

Or take the fundamental moral issues of our day— ranging from birth-control to death-control. The root of these questions is the same for Christians and non-Christians: what does it mean to be truly and responsibly human? There is no peculiarly Christian answer to them; and Christians, like others, will want to insist on differing —and divergent—emphases. That there is more agreement between some humanists and some Christians than between some Christians and other Christians is neither a surprise nor a condemnation. On almost any 'gut' issues I can think of—civil liberties, race, matters of life and death, sex, censorship, etc.—I would expect instinctively to find myself closer to some humanists I know than to many Christians I know.

This does not mean that Christianity makes no difference. There is—or should be—a difference of dimension in our estimate of man. In the light of Christ *both* the demand *and* the freedom of a genuinely human existence ought to appear a great deal more searching. It is if one or the other of these seems not to in a so-called Christian estimate that we should worry—if, that is to say, the demand is not costly or the freedom is stifled by a spirit of fear. Of course, too, there should be expected of Christians a morality that exceeds what can be expected (let alone enforced) in society as a whole. But it is not a different kind of morality. What distinguishes a Christian is not to be moral, any more than to be religious, in a particular way, but to be a man—with the radical obedience and freedom of Jesus Christ.

While I am stressing where the distinctiveness does *not* lie, let me mention one more source of misunderstanding—the relation of law to love. This constantly crops up in discussion of the so-called 'new morality'. What the advocates of this are *heard* to say is that non-Christians live under law but Christians live under love. But this is a serious misrepresentation. No responsible advocate of situational ethics denies law in favour of love or sees the two as antithetical. The real question is: For the truly human life now, is the place of law at the centre or the edge? Should law decide the moral issue or should it safeguard it? The paternalistic society and code morality (representing the stable state), which have had their Christian advocates just as much as their non-Christian, have said that in some things at least it should decide it—though most of these have a curious habit of turning out to do with sex! Abortion, for instance, is one of them. Even under our new legislation in Britain the moral (and not merely the medical) decision is taken by doctors, backed by judges. Rather, as in adoption, I am convinced that society should give the mother every encouragement, facility, *and therefore the real freedom,* to keep her child however unwanted; but finally the responsibility must be hers, since she has to carry it. The aim should be to *move towards* a mature society where the moral choice in issues of this sort (including sex relationships, divorce, euthanasia, gambling, drugs, reading-matter, and the rest) is taken by the individuals concerned and safeguarded by society against exploitation or abuse. The place of law —and as chairman of a law-reform society I am deeply concerned for good law—is at the edge to protect freedom, not at the centre to prohibit it. This I believe is a cardinal insight of the gospel, as true for non-Christians as for Christians, which then has to be translated, without any illusions about the selfishness and evil of man, into the moral leadership and legislative framework of a free, responsible, secular society—all to the end that life can be more deeply and truly human. And the idea that you can protect humanness, or love your neighbour, without getting involved in politics is so absurd that I don't propose to waste time on it.

So far I have tried to indicate where the distinctiveness of the Christian way does not lie. The aim, how to be human now (and it is an aim which is constantly expanding), should be the same for Christians and non-Christians. Of course it often isn't; and Christians have been sub-humanist as well as humanists sub-Christian. Yet there is equally insistently in the Gospels the call to a difference, to exceed the righteousness of the Scribes and Pharisees, to go beyond what the good pagan does. This comes out very clearly in some words of Jesus in St Luke's Gospel:

If you love only those who love you, what credit is that to you? Even sinners love those who love them.

Again, if you do good only to those who do good to you, what credit is that to you? Even sinners do as much. And if you lend only where you expect to be repaid, what credit is that to you? Even sinners lend to each other if they are to be repaid in full. But you must love your enemies and do good; and lend without expecting any return; and you will have a rich reward: you will be sons of the Most High, because he himself is kind to the ungrateful and wicked. Be compassionate as your Father is compassionate.[4]

These last words in St Matthew's version are, 'Be perfect, as your heavenly Father is perfect'.[5] I agree with those who think it likely that the Aramaic word lying behind both Greek translations meant 'whole', 'generous', 'gracious'. And it is this that is the basis of the appeal, 'What *charis*, what graciousness, have you?' What is truly human flows from that in which the human is founded. And here I believe we are at the heart of the real difference.

I said earlier that man is what he is open to. And the Christian understanding of what it means to be a man is to know oneself open not only to the environment of nature (where the rule is, Every man for himself) nor merely to the world of human rights (where the rule is, To each man his own) but to what St Paul summed up as 'the grace of our Lord Jesus Christ and the love of God and the fellowship of the Holy Spirit'. This is the *milieu divin* which alone truly creates the *zone humaine*. A Christian is one who testifies to this as the source and ground of the *humanum* for all—not only for Christians but for the ungrateful and the wicked.

The love of God—this is man's ultimate environment, what he is made from and what he is made for—'the beyond' which enables man, in the words of Gerhardt's lovely evening hymn, to

> Forget his selfish being,
>   For joy of beauty not his own.[6]

This is the basic difference between the Christian and the non-Christian humanist—that love is not only what ought to be the ultimate reality but what is. Herein is love: not that we love God—or man—but that he loves us. The whole of life is response to that prevenient presence, to which the openness is all. As Auden puts it with the poet's precision,

> Space is the Whom our loves are needed by,
> Time is our choice of How to love and Why.[7]

Yet this is frankly incredible. What evidence is there for such an estimate of the cosmos? What indeed, apart from the grace of our Lord Jesus Christ? Christians are distinguished by the conviction that we do here have a window through, a clearing in being, which enables us to trust that at heart being *is* gracious—not merely good as opposed to alien or absurd (as the most honest secular humanism from Thomas Huxley to Bertrand Russell and Camus has found it must assert), but accepting, forgiving. 'The unforgiving minute': that is how the hard world of time and space most usually strikes us. Indeed, there is really nothing in nature to suggest otherwise, which is why finally a nature mysticism cannot satisfy. The Christian way rests upon the logic, 'Freely you have received: freely give', 'Accept one another as Christ has accepted you', and, most fundamentally of all, 'Accept yourself—for you have been accepted'. There is ultimately nothing to worry about, nothing you have to be defensive about, nothing you can only secure by clinging. The Christian knows what every psychologist testifies, that we learn to love not by being told to love but by *being loved*. And it is this reality at the root of our humanness that the ultimacy of grace—or (viewed the other way round) the divinity of Christ—is affirming.

And then, thirdly, there is the fellowship of Holy Spirit. The Greek word *koinonia* here is an even more difficult one to define than love or grace. It means participation, having a share in, almost shares in, co-ownership. Its primary reference in the New Testament is not to fellowship between men (though if that doesn't follow it shows that you haven't got it) but to participation in the great encompassing, environmental reality of God, of Christ, and above all of Holy Spirit. This last is the very element of what the New Testament calls eternal life, as air is of biological life. Real living *is koinonia*: without it life cannot be whole, human, or holy. This is what the hippies are saying with their message of sharing, of be-ins and love-ins. And it's what others like them are insisting with regard to justice. To be without participation, economically or politically, is to be deprived, diminished, denied as human beings. The Christian way is essentially a social vision, what Teilhard de Chardin called 'a totally human hope'. Where *koinonia* is, wherever *koinonia* is, there is the Kingdom. Community is not to be identified with a community—let alone with the community of Christians. Holy community is a secular phenomenon for all men, to be celebrated where it is, wherever it is, and to be fought for where it isn't.

The distinctively Christian life-style is a way of living in the world which takes as basic these realities of the human condition, in the confidence that *nothing* in life or in death, in the world as it is or the world as it shall be, can finally defeat or separate from them. What it does *not* mean is living a distinct life. And the difference between these understandings has never been brought out better than in a classic description of the Christian way that goes back as far almost as the New Testament, to the anonymous Epistle to Diognetus in the second century. It ought to be as well known as anything in Scripture:

Christians are not distinguished from the rest of mankind either in locality or in speech or in customs. For they dwell not somewhere in cities of their own, neither do they use some different language, nor practise an extraordinary kind of life. . . . But while they dwell in cities of Greeks and barbarians as the lot of each is cast, and follow the native customs in dress and food and the other arrangements of life, yet the constitution of their own citizenship, which they set forth, is marvellous, and confessedly contradicts expectation. They dwell in their own countries, but only as sojourners; they bear their share in all things as citizens, and they endure all hardships as strangers. Every foreign country is a fatherland to them and every fatherland is foreign. . . . They obey the established laws and they surpass the laws in their own lives. . . . In a word, what the soul is in the body, this the Christians are in the world. . . . The soul is enclosed in the body, and yet itself holds the body together; so Christians are kept in the world as in a prison-house, yet they themselves hold the world together. . . . So great is the office for which God has appointed them, and which it is not lawful for them to decline.[8]

To the inside of this life-style I shall return in the fourth chapter. Our concern now is with its public marks. And from the outside they are mostly marks of paradox— of losing one's soul to save it, of identity through identification, freedom through service, resurrection through crucifixion. The Christian shows a baffling combination of attachment and detachment, of solidarity and non-conformity, commitment and openness. He cares more about this world than other men, and cares less: he may well give his life for it, but he will not give his life to it. He follows a master wholly at the mercy of men because he spared no cost, but never at the mercy of men because he had no price. St Paul piles on the apparent contradictions:

We are impostors who speak the truth, the unknown men whom all men know; dying we still live on; . . . poor ourselves, we bring wealth to many; penniless, we own the world.[9]

The First Epistle of Peter, too, supplies a fascinating glimpse (in 2: 11–17) of the Christian life-style, of living the Easter life in Nero's Rome (assuming it is by the apostle, which I think it is) within a few months of the conflagration which, like the Reichstag fire in Berlin, was made the excuse for rounding up the Christians. For sheer buoyancy and nerve you have to give it to them. There is not a hint of edginess or defensiveness. Freely they walk their tightrope with eyes open. Yet they know they are on a knife-edge from which at any moment they could slide to destruction.

First, says Peter, remember your situation: you're like aliens in a foreign country. He uses the word *paroikoi*, which has been domesticated to our 'parishioners', but which meant those on a residence permit, like foreign workers or temporary immigrants. And Christians in Rome knew the significance of that metaphor as keenly as any 'non-patrial' minority today. Only fifteen years before all Jews (and Christians like Aquila and Priscilla among them) had suddenly been deported from Rome at the edict of the Emperor Claudius. Men in this position know they have no security—their rights can be withdrawn at any time—and they know also that their behaviour will be scrutinized more searchingly than that of other groups. There are bound to be neighbours watching them and waiting to report anything untoward; and most allegations can be made to stick. And Christians are in this same vulnerable position. They are here on temporary papers: their citizenship is elsewhere. They must live their distinctive new life in the midst of this old world and its values. And between the two there is war. So watch it, says the Apostle, and give no handle to those who are looking for you to falter.

But he is not only negative. 'Let all your behaviour be such as even pagans can recognize as good'—so that even they will have to stand convicted. But here is the second knife-edge. For it's so easy to turn this into: 'Do what

they'll think is good. Adjust, accommodate, take your
standards from them, so that you don't stick out like a
sore thumb.' And there's no simple, guaranteed way of
telling the difference. It's a question of discernment, integrity, sensitivity. David Riesman in his book *The Lonely
Crowd* talks of the 'other-directed' man, who psycho-
logically and morally takes his cue from the crowd, who
follows the tail-lights of the car in front.[10] Yet Christians
are also other-directed men, in the sense that they are
followers of the man for others—constantly looking not
to themselves but to the needs of others. And the difference between these two at the moment of decision is
often paper-thin—though ultimately between them there
lies all the distance in the world.

And then, thirdly, there is the paradox of, 'Submit
yourselves to every human institution', *and*, 'Live as free
men'. Again, Christians are followers of the truly free
man—the one who was utterly free for God, free for
others, free for *all*. Yet nothing is further from Christian
freedom than the world's idea of a 'free for all'. Christian
liberty goes, not with bolshiness, but with due, and carefully discriminating, honour to all—love to the brother-
hood, reverence to God, respect to the sovereign and
government authorities. The Christian's life is a responsible life—and by his responsibility he is to 'put ignorance
and stupidity to silence'. Yet this does not mean mind-
less subservience—on the contrary. But, if you find yourself up against it (and it is clear that the Apostle has no
illusions), then be sure it is for well-doing rather than
for wrong. No one can say that this life-style is irrelevant
in a world torn between protest and conformity, and if it
can be lived in Nero's Rome, it can be lived in our
world.

And for a restatement of it for our day I cannot do
better than refer, all too briefly, to Ruben Alves's very
remarkable book, *A Theology of Human Hope*, written
out of the almost equally oppressive situation of con-

B

temporary Brazil. He characterizes the Christian life as
one of 'holy insecurity' in a 'totally secular world'—by
which he does not mean a 'profane' world, 'void of
transcendence', but one perpetually open in hope to the
power of God as constituting 'what it takes to make and
to keep life human in the world'. For the Christian, indeed, man lives this life as a marvellous gift, freely to
be enjoyed and savoured. Yet

> in the context of God's messianic politics of liberation
> the erotic sense of life exists only as it keeps man open
> for a new future. Life is there, to be eaten, but man is
> to eat it with bitter herbs, with his loins girt, his sandals
> on his feet, and he shall eat it in haste (see Exodus 12:
> 8–11). The bitter taste of suffering can never be elimi-
> nated from the 'aperitif', so that man will never settle
> for it.[11]

The Christian style of life has an elusiveness about it
that makes it impossible to pin down or define. It is not
marked by 'laws which never shall be broken'. For it
has no absolutes but love, and 'how to be loving now'
is not prescribed in advance. It is less concerned with
general standards than with specific stands. The Christian
finds himself saying with Luther, 'Here I stand. So help
me God, I can no other.' For there are constantly sticking points on which compromise is impossible, where
love, grace, *koinonia* are denied (and any form of
apartheid is by definition a denial of *koinonia*). Yet the
Christian way is free, supple, flexible, because it goes un-
erringly for the person rather than the principle, for man
rather than the sabbath. It is impossible to describe, in
the sense of drawing a circle round so that you can know
where you are and where your obligations cease. Yet it
is not hard to discern, in the sense that you can recognize
it when you see it. And the world *does* respond when it
sees it, in a Pope John or a Martin Luther King, a
Trevor Huddleston or a Helder Camara, a Daniel
Berrigan or a Camilo Torres, a César Chavez organizing

the grape-pickers of California or a Mother Teresa salvaging the dying of Calcutta—and in a nameless multitude of humbler examples.

The way doesn't need definition—nor even, in contrast to the truth, translation. For it is already in the common coin of love and justice, carrying a human image and superscription. The sole condition is that it be truly current coin, genuinely related to the great human questions of today. And this requires infinite sensitivity and unstinting presence, the identification of lives rather than of words. The way now is not, nor ever has been, metalled. Yet what Christians stand for—or, rather, the human things we stand for as Christians—*can* ring loud and clear. We have on the whole, thank God, seen that of late on the issues of race. There is *not* just hesitancy, doubt and confusion. This does not mean that there is agreement on policies—nothing has sifted Christians so searchingly as the World Council of Churches' grants to oppressed minorities. But the difference in being a Christian today, in style of life at least, is as marvellous, and frequently as contrary to expectation, as ever it was in the second century.

THREE

THE TRUTH—NOW

The most fundamental question about Christianity is not, Does it work? but, Is it true? And traditionally the most distinctive thing about Christianity has been not its way or its life but its beliefs—'quod ubique, quod semper, quod ab omnibus *creditum est*': what has always, everywhere and by every one been *believed*. But by the same canon 'the truth *now*' seems almost a contradiction. The way may change but surely not the truth, 'the everlasting gospel'. For is not Jesus Christ 'the same yesterday, today and for ever'?

If, as Dorothee Sölle, the German lay theologian, has put it,[1] the subject of theology were God alone, enthroned above the cherubim, then indeed the truth would not alter, and changes in theology (and in no subject, surprisingly, are books so quickly dated) would prove merely that we were dealing with passing human ideas masquerading as supernatural science. But Christian theology is about truth incarnate—and it must change with the world in which the truth has to be made flesh. For the Christian would agree with Lenin that 'truth is always concrete'. Jesus Christ is the same yesterday, today and for ever only by being the contemporary of each generation and therefore different for each generation. The Christ of the fifth, or the fifteenth, or the nineteenth century is not Christ for us today. Far more than theologians have been wont to acknowledge, Christianity is always changing, because the world is always changing: for it is about God *ad hominem*, God *pro nobis*—God related to man, God for us. In the words of the first wise man in Auden's Christmas oratorio,

To discover how to be *truthful now*
Is the reason I follow this star.

The question of truth is always for the Christian, as
Kierkegaard insisted, an existential one. His is not simply
Pilate's question, 'What is truth?', but, 'What is my rela-
tion to the truth, what is true for me?'

This is reflected in the fact that all the statements in
the Creed are dependent on the words 'I [or we] believe
in'. They are statements not about timeless propositions
but persons in relationship. Yet there has been a constant
tendency in Christian theology to purchase objectivity by
abstracting from this personal relationship. As the so-
called Athanasian Creed puts it, 'This is the Catholick
Faith . . . which except every one do keep whole and undefiled without doubt he shall perish everlastingly.' There
are the grand certainties for you! That's what's meant by
'knowing where you stand', by the hard centre to which
we are exhorted to get back. And what is wrong with it?
Simply that the invitation has become one to concur rather
than to explore. The truth has been abstracted from the
relationship to experience—and for this reason has gone
dead. It lacks that vital quality which the journalist Paul
Ferris in his book *The Church of England* aptly called
'resonance'.[2] This is that indefinable something that makes
the truth feel lived in, that turns a house into a home.
And in the early 1960s he rightly detected it in the words
of my predecessor as Dean of Trinity, Harry Williams,
who was later to express it himself in the preface to his
book *The True Wilderness*: 'I resolved that I would not
preach about any aspect of Christian belief unless it had
become part of my own life-blood.'[3]

That statement has often been taken for subjectivism,
like Kierkegaard's dictum that 'truth is subjectivity'. But
it is not. It is a statement about how to be truthful. What
St John recognized in Jesus was the Word '*full* of grace
and *truth*'. What so many people sense in us are words

not truth-ful but hollow, no longer made flesh but the
shells with the fish gone out of them. People find them
presented as given truths and do not know what to make
of them, for they are answers that have not been shaped
by their questions. The structure of Christian doctrine, as
Donald Schon said of the U.S. Federal Government, is
like 'a series of memorials to old problems'. The 'deposit'
of truth once delivered to the saints now sounds less like
something laid down (like wine) than something washed
up (like silt): the metaphor has subtly shifted.

Here, I believe, lies the real challenge to the Church's
credibility today. It is not that men accuse us of lying—
though the charge of hypocrisy dies hard. It is still true,
as Alec Vidler said nearly ten years ago, that 'we've got
a very big leeway to make up, because there's been so
much suppression of real, deep thought and intellectual
alertness and integrity in the Church.'[4] But that, thank
God, is surely better now. No, today it is that men wonder
whether, even to us, our words mean *anything*: they seem
hollow. If they hold these empty shells to their ears, will
their contact with 'the sea of faith' be only now to hear,
like Matthew Arnold standing on Dover beach, 'its
melancholy, long, withdrawing roar'?

Let me illustrate this gap between doctrine and
experience. I spoke earlier of the love of God and the
grace of our Lord Jesus Christ and the fellowship of Holy
Spirit as the great existential realities at the heart for the
Christian of what it means to be human now. And it is
this central, pulsing reality that the doctrine of the Trinity
is about. Yet no formulation strikes men as more dessi-
cated or remote. And the answer is not to summon people
to their feet and announce rousingly Cardinal Newman's
hymn:

> Firmly I believe and truly
>   God is three and God is one;
> And I next acknowledge duly
>   Manhood taken by the Son.[5]

The mathematics seems totally unapplied and the little word 'duly' speaks volumes. And so one could go on. The doctrine of the Atonement, as Rosemary Haughton has brilliantly illustrated in her books, *On Trying to be Human* and *The Transformation of Man*,[6] is actually about the transformation of human relationships here and now. But it doesn't appear to be: it seems to be about some distant divine-human transaction on 'a green hill far away', of which people *begin* by asking, 'How on earth could this affect me?'

Experience of discussion over the past ten years has convinced me that for ordinary men and women the Creed, the deposit of the truth, is even more remote than the code or the cultus, the traditional markers of the way and the life—and that is saying a good deal. 'Theology' is regarded as mere theory unrelated to the real business of life. It's so much 'God-talk'—not false, but what in the eyes of this generation is almost worse: unfalsifiable. Nowhere is the demand more insistent: Put up or shut up. And by 'put up' is meant: come up with (what Roger Garaudy, the French Marxist, calls) 'the flesh of your God', the living, trembling stuff of which Christian truth is made.

Let us at this point go back to source. Why did the early Christians make the response: '*full* of grace and truth'? Because in Jesus they recognized someone who spoke 'with authority', that is, as the root of the word in Latin implies, from source, or, in the Greek, *ex-ousia*, from being. In Jesus's case there was no gap. He was transparently credible: he knew of what he spoke, he was authentic, he had been there. Indeed he could be represented by those who knew him as saying, 'I *am* the truth'. Truth was made flesh in front of them: to have seen him *was* to have seen the Father.

And this supplies the clue to the way in for us—the flesh now. The test, says St John, of what is authentically and distinctively Christian is Jesus Christ come and coming in the flesh. And this test is not confined to the past: it relates to the Christ who is in the world as we are in the world—embodied in people. The starting-point still is flesh and blood, and the movement is from relationships to revelation, from experience to authority, from Christ as man to Christ as God.

Yet it is precisely this transition from man-talk to God-talk that today is problematical. For, as Fred Brown has put it, who was recently thrown out of the Salvation Army in Britain over the censorship of his book *Secular Evangelism*, 'God is a language-barrier'. The very word belongs to another world. Theology was once defined by Paul Tillich as taking rational trouble about a mystery. But there are thousands today who cannot recognize the mystery (*theos*) because of the language (*logos*). This is the truth behind the 'death of God' theologians. This three-letter word, 'God', they are saying, has had it. Yet they insist on calling themselves theologians. They are not just atheists. And it is no good replying with a lapel-button, 'God is alive and well in Austin, Texas'. Perhaps he is there, and for many who still believe in the stable state. But he is sick and tired in a lot of other places.

I don't personally believe that the word 'God' *is* finally dead. Ultimately I doubt if we can get on without it (or some other like it) for designating *and grounding* the recurrent awarenesses of transcendence in experience. I would agree with the judgement of Langdon Gilkey of Chicago, in his book *Naming the Whirlwind*:

> To leave these supremely significant areas of our existence unsymbolized, unpondered, and so uncomprehended, is to leave secular life impoverished with regard to its real values, and vulnerable with regard to its real fears. Religious discourse is essential if secular life is to achieve a creative worldliness.[7]

But I am entirely prepared to accept that we should not start with the word 'God', and I'd happily settle for a moratorium or close season on its use. After all, Jesus, for whom God-language was no problem, used it remarkably little in talking to the crowds. 'You want to know what the kingdom of God is like?' 'Well, it's like this.' And then he'd describe some ordinary scene from human life in which 'God' didn't apparently feature at all—such as a businessman doing a deal for hidden treasure, or a woman hunting for a missing coin, or a bailiff cooking the accounts.

Or take the parable of the good Samaritan. 'God' is never mentioned. Yet it would be a great mistake to assume that it's just about the horizontal relationships of life, the closed world of secular human*ism*. Where then is God? Primarily of course he is represented in the figure who embodies *agape*, the utterly uncalculating love shown by the Samaritan. This man indeed is a sort of Christ-figure—and some have seen here a pen-portrait of Jesus, drawn perhaps from life. But the point of the parable is that the Christ-figure is *any* man who makes love flesh in the here and now. The story starts indeed from the question, 'Who is my neighbour?', which in the lawyer's mind is really the question, 'Who is *not* my neighbour, where can I draw the line?'—which is why it can't be answered. Instead the parable ends with another question, 'Who *proved* neighbour?', redefining neighbour in terms of the subject not the object of the action. But notice, it does *not* say, 'You shouldn't be starting from neighbour at all—that's mere humanism—but from God.' And this is important for us. For man's immediate question today is not Luther's question, 'Where may I find a gracious God?', and the answer is not, 'God loves you'. Tell that, said Fred Brown, to the hippies and drug-addicts in Soho and it would seem to them a sick joke—*as it would have to the man who fell among thieves*. His question, as the life-blood drains from him, is, 'Where may I find a gracious neighbour?', literally, 'Who will draw near?' Yet the answer to the question, 'Where may I find a gracious neighbour?', and to the question, 'Where may I

find a gracious God?', is for the Christian the same—
the man Christ Jesus. You can come at it either way. For
Christianity has a radically incarnate view of truth. This
is what in his day Augustine saw distinguished it from
that of the Platonists: the Word has been made *flesh*.
God *is* that by which he is represented (what Norman
Pittenger calls his 'surrogate')—namely, love: for 'he
who dwells in love is dwelling in God, and God in him'.
At the heart of the gospel, and therefore of Christian
doctrine, is a double pattern of representation: 'Whoever
receives the least of these, receives me; and whoever
receives me, receives not me but him who sent me'.[8]
Where love is, Christ is; and where Christ is, God is.

But what is the meaning, the status, of this 'is', when
we say, God *is* that by which he is represented? Primarily
it is functional: this is how it works out in practice. For
the Bible, like modern secular man, has a very functional
view of truth. 'Did not your father', says Jeremiah, 'do
justice and righteousness? . . . He judged the cause of the
poor and needy . . . *Is not this to know me? says the
Lord*'.[9] Similarly St John speaks of '*doing* the truth'; and
it is he who 'does the will' that shall 'know of the
doctrine'.[10] For as Bonhoeffer paraphrased it, 'We shall
never know what we do not do'. But it is not a merely
functional or pragmatic view of truth, in the sense that it
denies the metaphysical or says that we can never say
anything about how things really are: for this, and none
other, *is* the way into *how things are*.

On the philosophical status of that 'is' there is no doubt
a vast amount more to say—an indefinite field for research
into the meaning of 'God' language. That is for those who
can take it. Yet *all* can start here, with the flesh now.
This is the point of the chapter headings in Fred Brown's
book. The word 'God' may be vacuous—yet God *is*
Astonished Joy, God *is* Community, Responsibility,
Fulfilment (or Freedom from Fear). For in real meeting
and giving of yourself you do encounter that to which

the tag 'God' has been attached. And 'this is for real, man'—even if, as in the parable of the sheep and the goats, you do not 'know', and indeed disclaim any meeting with God or Christ, saying with surprise, 'But, Lord, when did we see you?' Yet if they saw but didn't know, it's all right. The real denial of Christ in the flesh is not that he is not named but that he is not represented—that there is no surrogate of love. And the crucial test is not whether you have said, 'Lord, Lord', but how much you have loved. At the end of the day, for the New Testament, it will not matter if a man says to Christ, 'I never knew you'; it will matter very much if Christ says that to him. That is why, in a tradition going back to St Augustine, deeply orthodox believers like Karl Rahner have spoken of 'anonymous Christians' or Paul Tillich of 'the latent Church' or Dorothee Sölle of 'the Church outside the Church'; and Fred Brown has even said, 'There are more Christians outside than inside the Church'.

Yet once more we are back at the question, What then is the difference? And there is, I believe, a genuine source of misunderstanding here. What is a Christian? We really need a separate name for the son (as the parable puts it) who *says*, 'I go', and for the son who goes. There is no doubt that it is the going rather than the saying which is decisive, but no doubt also that in New Testament usage Christians are distinguished by acknowledging Christ, by naming him. They are those who 'believe in their heart and confess with their lips that Jesus is Lord'. *Just* to say, 'Lord, Lord', is fruitless. But to say, 'Lord', is an essential mark of being a Christian. As St Paul put it at Athens, 'What you worship but do not know—this is what I . . . proclaim.'[11] And the function of 'God' and 'Christ' language is precisely to identify the otherwise nameless, ineffable experience.

Yet the naming is always secondary to the experience, never the decisive thing. Indeed it may trail a long way behind the experience, often leaving Christians standing

while others are instinctively seized of the reality and
'do the will'. The recognition that leads to the acknowledgement and naming is a matter of spotting the incognito,
of blurting out, pointing helplessly, and saying, 'Look,
don't you *see*?' A Dutchman (Cornelius van Peursen) has
written on God under the title *Him Again*,[12] to bring out
that for the Bible, and particularly for the Old Testament,
theology is more like train-spotting than poring over a
celestial time-table. The men of the Bible found they
had experiences in the ordinary course of nature which
took them out of themselves, and then they reflected, 'God
was in this place—and I did not know it'. And constantly
that mysterious presence seemed to be recurring in their
history—'the God of Abraham' they called it; and later
'the God of Isaac'; and later 'the God of Jacob'. And
eventually they realized, 'It's the same each time. It's HIM
again.' And they gave him the mysterious name that keeps
its own secret, 'I am who I am',[13] or, in Martin Buber's
suggestive translation, 'I shall be there as I shall be
there'. Identifying him was rather like tracing a series of
crimes with features in common; and out of widely
assorted experiences they built up a kind of human identi-
kit of God, a Christ-figure—misleading at many points,
yet enough to recognize your man when you see him.
And in Jesus they said, 'That's it. He's the one. Now we
know who's behind it all.'

Yes, Christians are those who name God—by pointing to the man. They certainly don't claim to define God,
to know what he connotes, what he is in himself; only
what he denotes, what he's like if you meet him. The
truth, like the way and the life, is in the experienced
relationship, not in the name. And they are more concerned (or should be) that men should share the reality
than name the name. Indeed, if that gets in the way, they
can get by without God-language (after all the Jews did
who refused to take his name upon their lips at all or
allow *any* image of God). *Having put up, they can shut*

up: with the reality to touch and see and handle, how we say it in words is much less important. 'On the boundaries', said Bonhoeffer, 'it is better to hold our peace', and the boundaries of shared terms with humanists and others in our culture for *talking* about the things of the spirit are narrower today than they were. Indeed, St Augustine said ages ago of the Trinity that one must speak only because by silence one might seem to deny.

But let me end by insisting, as I did in relation to the way, that this reticence does not mean vagueness or confusion, any more than it did for St Augustine. Faith, as Ian Ramsey, the Bishop of Durham, said in his opening address to the last Lambeth Conference, is precisely the ability to live with uncertainty. I referred in my opening chapter to an article in the *Daily Mail*, by one Peter Lewis, which spoke of the Pope and the Archbishop of Canterbury as 'two elderly and puzzled men . . . who no longer represent anything but doubt and confusion'. It appeared merely snide and negative, and I read it only because it was sent to me by a parson to 'answer'. But at its close it returned to doubt in a way that suggested something positive to which I think we should listen:

The religion that survives, if any does, is going to have to be a religion of doubt. . . . A new human idea of God is struggling to be born. When that changes, all must change with it, however fiercely people bid the waves retreat. Of course, men could throw out the idea of God altogether, as many have tried to do, in order to worship something tangible. The favourite candidate at present is the Gross National Product, a new and uglier name for a very old god, Mammon. But the religious instinct, which is as old as man, rests on the conviction that there is more in human life than Mammon, that there is more than what is visible. Theology is the search for the invisible factor, called God, which is always changing and evolving with man's consciousness. It is surely this which the Pope and the Arch-

bishop should be talking about. It is this Church whose
doors they should be opening, where men and women
could enter together as intelligent seekers and wor-
shippers, instead of custodians of old habits and dis-
carded ideas.[14]

Well, discount the journalistic edge, discount the notion
that the new ideas and the old Church are merely at logger-
heads, and I believe there *is* something here about being
truthful now. To those who trust still in the stable state it
may sound dangerously humanistic—though I am constantly astonished by Christian friends who seem more
worried by a human than an inhuman idea of God. But
the 'new human idea of God . . . always changing and
evolving with man's consciousness' I take to be comple-
mentary not antithetical to what Barth called 'the
humanity of God' constantly seeking anew to be made
flesh as the contemporary of each generation. We 'have'
indeed, as St John insists, Jesus Christ come and coming
in the flesh. That for Christians is the touchstone of truth.
'We know that the Son of God has come and given us
understanding to know him who is real; indeed we are
in him who is real, since we are in his Son Jesus Christ.'[15]
But he is not an 'idea of God'. *That,* the way of express-
ing it for the mind or the imagination, must change, and,
thank God, is changing—otherwise we should be stagnant.

Furthermore, I think we must be open to the fact—
whether we like it or not—that commitment to Christ
and the 'idea of God' in *any* form are for many of our
contemporaries antithetical. This is the thesis of Alistair
Kee's impressively argued Pelican book, *The Way of
Transcendence,* which carries the sub-title *Christian Faith
without Belief in God.* The call to faith, for him, is to
'commitment, with ultimate concern, to that which came
to expression in Jesus Christ',[16] that is, to a way of freedom, transcending and cutting across the merely natural
and selfish—which means inevitably also the way of the
cross. To make belief in a supernatural being a precondi-

tion of being a Christian is, he argues, the equivalent today of requiring a form of circumcision. For this belief has for cultural reasons *become* a stumbling block that previously it never was (once everyone accepted it naturally) and is in danger of displacing the real offence of the gospel, Jesus Christ and him crucified. It must be cleared out of the way, not in order to make Christianity palatable but precisely to expose its true challenge.

I believe that we must take this position seriously— for I am sure that Kee has the pulse of many of the young, and not so young. For myself I am persuaded that this insistent call to 'go beyond', to refuse to rest in 'what comes naturally', is, like men's other responses to reality, rational and justified in so far as it is called out by the nature of their environment. If this is the 'right' way to live, is there no corresponding spiritual reality that *evokes* this restlessness, and ultimately satisfies it? In other words, I am still convinced that the reality of God, how- ever conceived, is an *implication* of 'the way of transcen- dence'. But I am sure that no idea of God, particularly not the crude traditional one of 'a supernatural being', should be made its *precondition*. Yet this, says Kee not unjustifiably, is what the Churches at any rate appear from the outside to be insisting on: Jesus cannot be had on any other terms.

I would wish to welcome his plea for 'pluralism'[17] which he dismisses, with regret, as 'too unrealistic for words'), that is, for creative coexistence within the Church of divergent positions. For if the Churches are really unable to incorporate and learn from those who want to be Christians but cannot get on with God language, then we shall all be impoverished. For it is not only the line be- tween the two life-styles, but the line between the two languages, that runs, if we are honest, through the midst of each of us: at different times we find ourselves on either side of it. We *need* the 'latent theology' as well as the 'latent Church', to keep us Christian. For the official containers, verbal and institutional, are in peril of extruding as much as they include.

This, of course, is an offence—it should not be—though not so great an offence as rejecting one of these little ones. There is, I believe, especially today, more danger in a static doctrinal fundamentalism than in most heresy. But to be 'truthful *now*' to what may be required in thought or action is not for me a signal to abandon Christianity. It is a signal to grow and to explore. And that, in the deepest sense of the words, is 'the *reason* I *follow* this star'.

FOUR

THE LIFE—NOW

'These things are written', said St John of his Gospel, 'that you may believe, and that believing you may have *life*.'[1] The way and the truth are for the sake of the life— 'eternal life', which does not simply mean life after death, but real life, at a depth and of a quality that nothing merely biological can either give or take away. Of course it includes life after death—it simply would not be what it is if it could be finished by a bacillus or a bus. But it is life beyond self in every sense of the word.

Just as Christianity is referred to in Acts as 'the way', so it is described as 'this life'. The life is the inside of the way. The way is a style of relationship to the world, and is primarily marked by doing. The life is the inner secret of the style, and is primarily marked by being. What then is the distinctively Christian life—now, individually and corporately?

One has only to use the phrase 'the Christian life', and consider what it is contrasted with, to recognize that hitherto it has presupposed a pretty simple, uncomplicated version of the centre-periphery model. In this model, Christ is at the centre of a circle of light. The innermost ring comprises churchmen who are faithfully trying to live 'the Christian life' (saying their prayers, going to church, receiving the sacraments, and so on). Thence there is a shading off to nominal, 'four-wheeler' Christians (who come to church in their pram to be christened, in the taxi to be married, and in the hearse to be buried), to those on the fringe, and finally to outsiders (who live in the darkness of 'the world'). On this view there is a simple equation: to join the Church is to come into the life and to come into the life is to join the Church. 'The life' is a world of its own within the world—variously characterized as 'the spiritual life', 'the sacramental life', even 'church life' (as in the phrase, 'How is church life in your town?'). It is opposed to the world's life, as the religious to the secular.

And the same model has served structurally as well as spiritually. The Church has been thought of as *a* community within *the* community, an *imperium in imperio*, a sort of miniature Vatican City in every place, with its own centre and its own life built up round it—over against the life of the world which it seeks to influence, and if possible control, from that centre. A good example of this, from the very source of the model, was the recent attempt of the Vatican to prevent divorce in Italy. And significantly it failed. Indeed, if this is the model, then as secularization spreads the Church must expect to live in constant retreat, being pushed back to the ghetto or tolerated as a picturesque part of the old city. The model really only works on the assumptions that obtained in the period we now know as Christendom—that Church and State were theoretically co-terminous and that salvation meant being in the Church. But this was a quite exceptional pattern. It is nowhere even dreamt of in the New Testament; and it presupposed a pre-secular society, mass conversion, and above all the backing of the Church by the power of the State. Yet many in the Church still hanker after a return to this ideal—like churchwardens who tell you that we must keep the pews for 'when they come back'. And we still try to operate a parochial system adapted to it—even if the new town, and still more the new megalopolis, has long since outgrown the old city and reduced it spiritually to an island site where 'the Christian life' is preserved.

But I believe we must question this model of the life for the same reason that we questioned it as a model of the way. For, as the writer of the Epistle to Diognétus said, 'Christians do not live in cities of their own'—even spiritual cities. The Christian life is not distinctive by being distinct: it does not mean 'separate development', a life within life, whether it be in the enclosed garden of the soul or the gathered fellowship of the congregation.

Rather, the question of the life is the question of 'how to be living now'—as opposed to partly living. Real living: this is what the gospel is about, how to 'have life', abundant life, how to come alive in every dimension of one's being—what the New Testament calls 'alive to God', totally open to the infinite possibilities of being 'human now'. And this life, St John insisted, is 'life for the world',[2] not only life for the Church or in the Church. The life is 'the light of men', of 'every man coming into the world';[3] it is the secret of what it means to be human, not to be religious in a particular way. And what distinguishes a Christian is that he says with St Paul, 'To me to live is *Christ*':[4] for here—not only in the historical Jesus but in all that is meant by the new being 'in Christ' —he sees life defined and vindicated with a richness and a power that he does not see in Zen, or the Tao, or the Torah, or Marxism, however much all these and others may have to offer.

And the gospel is concerned with how men may 'enter life', 'find life'. And these phrases stand parallel in the New Testament not with entering the Church but with entering the Kingdom. This is not to depreciate the Church —to its essential place I shall return. But, to be true to the Bible, one must expound the life, like the way of which it is the secret, as primarily something worldly, secular. It is common life uncommonly good, ordinary life transformed into something extra-ordinary. We catch ourselves saying sometimes, 'This is the life!'—when perhaps even momentarily existence becomes blissful, transfigured, shared. And this is what more and more people are realizing today escapes them. There is a revolt against the world we have to live in because it doesn't give life but death. Here as elsewhere there is revolution of rising expectations. There is a quest on all sides for quality of life, expansion of consciousness and sensitivity, maturity of relationship, release of the human potential. The concern is for the exploration of inner space, of love, tenderness, togetherness, wholeness, the total environment of man. All this, as we know, can lead to a new kind of subculture, with its own opium for the people, a privatized world, a-political and other-worldly. But it need not, and indeed a primary witness of the gospel today is surely to insist that it must not.

For Christian spirituality is about the inside of a worldly life. The Christian, said Bonhoeffer, 'must live a secular life, and thereby share in God's sufferings'.[5] But first, he insisted, the gospel is that 'he *may* live a secular life'. You *can* be identified, totally, in love, without losing identity, because 'your life is hid with Christ in God'. This is the meaning of the 'secret discipline' which for Bonhoeffer was the essential complement of 'religionless Christianity'. This is the clue to secular sainthood—what Dag Hammarskjöld, a notable unchurched example of it, spoke of in his *Markings* as 'freedom in the midst of action, stillness in the midst of other human beings'.[6] This is the inner freedom which the Gospels depict of Jesus. And it is gained not by cutting oneself off (however indispensable the rhythm of withdrawal) but by what Kierkegaard called 'a deeper immersion in existence' or Luther described as 'drawing Christ deeper into the flesh'. The Christian life is essentially an *embodied* life, a social life. 'Hereby we know that we have passed from death to life, because we love our brothers.'[7] And Monica Furlong offers the same test of a true mysticism in her book, *Travelling In*:

> We will know that we are more or less on the trade route when we want, at least some of the time, to be generous and loving. When we find ourselves hating or taking up astrology, we shall need to see whether we have been misled by a mirage.[8]

There is something wrong, to use Harry Williams's

analogy, if we can only live the new life in an oxygen cylinder—if we cannot breathe the smoke-filled air of the saloon but only the smoke-filled air of the sanctuary.' I am not against holy smoke: I even prefer it to the other (though try the *combination* of incense and cigars for heaven!), and no one has yet proved its connection with cancer. Yet if the holy life becomes a proxy for living, or Holy Communion for human communion, then we are lost. For the spiritual life *is* life at the level of spirit; Holy Communion *is* community made holy; liturgy *is* life 'lived up', celebrated, made new in the kingdom of God.

Then what room is there for the particular holy place or holy time? What is the role of the Church, of the group 'called out', the *ec-clesia*? Has it all been a mistake?

First, whatever else it is, the Church is not a substitute for the world. Yet on the old model it was presupposed that ideally the Church would become a replacement for the world—the world, hopefully, would become the Church. For life, eternal life, was in the Church, and the Church's proper concern therefore was to bring all men into itself, because this was to be 'saved'. The corollary was that outside the Church there was no salvation. And even if God was not bound by this logic, men were. The motive and goal of Christian mission (if you were a Catholic) was to baptize all men before they died or (if you were a Protestant) to convert all men before they died. Otherwise they might be damned everlastingly. Certainly there was no assurance that they would be saved. Even in the early decades of this century 'the evangelization of the world in this generation' was seen as a measured target. It was never really doubted that the object of evangelism was to make all men Christians, which for Roman Catholics meant quite simply make all men Roman Catholics—and the same for others *mutatis mutandis*, with varying discounts according to the hardness of your theology or the breadth of your charity.

Now this idea has got gradually—but rather rapidly—

eroded. And if this is the logic of evangelism, then indeed the Christian mission is in a mess—and those are right who fear that 'the new theology' cuts the nerve of missionary motive. Yet we have—or should have—no less concern for men if we don't expect to make them Episcopalians, or even Christians. We may even have a more genuine and disinterested concern (I am reminded of the Texan bishop who is reported to have had on his calling-card, 'Drive carefully. You may run over an Episcopalian'). Indeed, I believe the Church is being freed to exist for others in a new way—like the Good Shepherd to lay down *its* life for the world.

Hitherto we have talked as though the object of the Church in relation to the community was to impress *its* way of life on the community and to draw the community into *it*—because, as I said, fundamentally Christ was to be found in it and not in the world. But I believe we have to re-ask the question of the Church in a more fundamental form: What is the relation of *ecclesia*, being called out, to *koinonia*, community or participation?

Koinonia is where the Kingdom is, and the Kingdom is where *koinonia* is, in the world—whether in mercy or judgement. *Ecclesia* is whatever formation is called for in a particular situation to meet the claims of *koinonia*, to embody life, love, justice, freedom—in other words to make life human. *Ecclesia* is originally in Greek a secular word, standing for any assembly or gathering of people, and it is a pity that its use has come to be confined to the ecclesiastical, to the Christian Church as a religious organization. As Ignatius said back at the beginning, *ubi Christus ibi ecclesia*, wherever the Christ takes shape there is the Church (though the established model has reversed this to 'where the Church is, there is Christ'). And 'the clusters called for' (which is the root meaning of *ecclesia*) to make life human will be composed of many who cannot 'name' him but who are just as concerned for *koinonia* in such basic human issues as the supply and distribution of bread, civil liberties, race, peace, pollution, population control, literacy, law reform, minority rights, etc., etc. These problems do not require a specifically Christian answer any more than those that faced the good Samaritan. Indeed the whole point of Jesus's parable was precisely that what needed to be done could be done by non-churchmen, who might frequently judge churchmen (the priest and the levite) in this regard.

Yet there would be no judgement if this were not above all where Christians should be—in *ecclesia*. (It's interesting how the New Testament uses this phrase without the article and how ludicrously diminished it is by our translation 'in church'!) For Christians should be in the 'special relationship' which *ecclesia* or being called out implies—not of privilege but of conscious commitment. This is the truth of the saying that you can't be a Christian without being a member of the Church—which is still compatible with there being more Christians, more people who really have the heart of the matter, outside the religious organization than in it. To be in *ecclesia* is to respond to the call to servanthood, to accept special responsibility for the life of the Kingdom, for embodying *koinonia*. And the Christian does this basically because he cannot help it. As St Paul puts it, 'The love of Christ leaves us no choice.'[10] And the testimony of Christian generations is that 'this [above all] is the life'—for thus to serve is to reign, truly to be free. But it is *not* because only in the Church is there life, as if this were the exclusive locus of salvation. It is because the life made articulate, consciously and corporately appropriated, can be richer and deeper, freer and more joyful, than when it is lived with some levels of the personality not engaged.

Christians can be much more relaxed about the Church, without the frenzied concern to get people in or be damned. The Church is missionary, not primarily because it is trying to pull people into itself (this is proselytism—whose root meaning is 'come to us'), but because it is constantly reaching beyond itself—with the call, 'Come with us'. A Christian *will* be concerned for making more Christians, because he believes that the Kingdom, the revolution, being human now, desperately needs men and women prepared to make explicit commitment: it needs people prepared for the cost, in Marxist terms, of joining the party. But this concern is a by-product of his being turned outwards towards the world, of seeking first the kingdom of God. Those *not* called to this special relationship of being in the Church (and they will always apparently be in the great majority—if the Bible, right through to the Book of the Revelation, is any guide) are not *for that reason* condemned—though they may be for other reasons, which have to do with lovelessness.

Ecclesia is a function of *koinonia*—grouping is called out by participation: *koinonia* is not a function of *ecclesia* —so that you have to join the Church to find fellowship. That is the heart of the 'Copernican revolution' of which Richard McBrien, the American Roman Catholic, speaks in his very radical book, *Do We Need the Church?*[11] and which he says has now got to be joined *at the same time* with an 'Einsteinian revolution'—the recognition that *no* church (and no pope) enjoys an absolute perspective. But the Copernican revolution is the basic one—and if we get that right the rest will look after itself.

For what the world needs, what humanity requires, is not (as Bonhoeffer put it) 'the attempt to rescue the Church as an institution for salvation',[12] but Kingdom-men prepared for *any* kind of ecclesial structure. And at this point more than anywhere else we are watching the end of the stable state. In a world of crumbling statistics I have every sympathy (as a bishop) with Church leaders and with ordinary Church members. It *is* very bewildering. Things are literally all over the place. The centre-periphery model is yielding to new processes of learning and response, new forms of ministry, new patterns of Christian presence— epitomized by the para-church alongside the established

structures. But I am convinced that there will continue to
be much overlap and that the new will not be related
purely negatively to the old: for I am constitutionally a
both-and rather than an either-or man. Yet the result will
be a looser, more open texture, with growth and change
tending to move from the edges inwards rather than the
other way round. Describing this model in other areas of
life Donald Schon said this:

> It's a kind of amoeba, with very unclear boundaries,
> with no clear centre, with no clear structure, but with
> a very powerful, informal, interpersonal network that
> pulls the whole thing together.

It sounds chaotic and hopeless. But

> not only does it survive but it turns out to be darn
> near invulnerable. . . . There is nothing to strike at.[13]

I do not propose here to pursue the possible patterns
of this life, whether in prayer or liturgy, ministry or
organization.[14] But let me just say this. The life is going to
have to be available loose and not only packaged. For
fewer and fewer will buy it in the old containers. And
let me illustrate this from the great sign or sacrament of
life in the Christian tradition, the breaking and sharing
of bread—though it is a sad commentary on the dichotomy
in Christian history that the two bodies with the best
public record for social witness, the Quakers and the
Salvation Army, are the two who see no need for the
sacrament. For it has been carefully confined to the
Church: to enjoy this life you must come inside the glass-
case of its sanctuaries and its disciplines. And, absolutely
rightly, it has been stressed above all as *the* sacrament of
koinonia, of fellowship and unity. The individualism of
'making my communion' and the unchurchliness of casual
intercommunion are indeed fearful denials of it. But increasingly I become concerned whether we are not denying it just as much by ecclesiasticism, by making, at this
point above all, *koinonia* a function of *ecclesia* rather
than vice versa.

For the Eucharist is not simply an ecclesiastical
ordinance. It was instituted by Jesus at the Last Supper as
a sign and pledge of the Kingdom—a foretaste of a new
world. And this receives great emphasis in the longest
treatment of it in the New Testament, when in St John's
Gospel—arising directly out of the mass feeding in the
desert—Jesus is made to say: *'Whoever* comes to me . . .
I will never turn away'; 'if *anyone* eats this bread he shall
live'; 'the bread which I will give is . . . for the life of the
world'.[15] John Wesley surely had hold of a truth when he
described this love feast as a 'converting ordinance'—as
long as we remember, as Fred Brown says in his subsequent book *Faith without Religion,* that the Church's
first concern is not with making converts but with making
people (though the two *should* of course be synonymous).[16]
The Eucharist is not only for nourishing life but for creat-
ing it.

This really came home to me at a celebration (in every
sense of the word) which broke most of the Church rules
but which I believe was a great sacrament of life. It was
an open-air gathering in the foothills of California at a
sort of Franciscan haven for hippies and flower-children
and other drop-outs. The clergy present were about half-
and-half Anglican and Roman Catholic, with Kilmer
Myers, the Episcopal Bishop of California, presiding, a
Trappist abbot preaching, and *everyone* communicating.
Dressed in ordinary clothes with an Indian flower garland
round my neck (quite the most fragrant vestment I have
ever worn) I had among others the task of dispensing the
wafer breads, which in the evening breeze were in constant
peril of being scattered broadcast upon the mountains.
Among the milling mass coming up for communion was
what I could sense was a very regular Episcopalian family
with their two children. The kids looked anxiously at
their parents expecting to be passed over because they
weren't confirmed. Whereupon I knew I had to say, 'Come
on, everybody's getting it tonight'. And, after receiving.

the four hugged each other with a joy that almost made you weep. That was life for the world! And the whole thing was a miracle of sharing, more like the feeding of the five thousand than anything I have experienced. It was not individualistic indiscipline—far from it: it was a great act of *koinonia*. But it was the life, Christian life, breaking loose and denying only what denied life. And to deny life is so often the effect today of the old containers.

The 'happening' I have cited was exceptional in that it was fairly large, but little happenings in *ad hoc* surroundings are likely more and more to be the norm. This doesn't mean they will supersede the formal structures or the regular occasions; but people will take life where they find it—in church and out. And the life itself will refuse to be entombed. It's not that we have to strive officiously to keep it alive. It will break out. For as a Christian I believe in life as resurrection. That doesn't mean I'm optimistic. Like so many who are concerned to think and work for change, I feel increasingly alienated from the mind (or mindlessness) of the Establishment, though a good deal more, of late, in State than in Church—judges induce even more despair than bishops! There is less of a spirit of freedom abroad than a spirit of fear and frustration. And, as John F. Kennedy said, 'Those who make peaceful revolution impossible will make violent revolution inevitable.' I am not optimistic, but I am hopeful. For, thank God, there is another power at work. In the words of Sydney Carter's song,

> They cut me down
> And I leap up high—
> I am the life
> That'll never, never die.
> I'll live in you
> If you'll live in me.
> I am the Lord
> Of the dance, said he.[17]

'I have tried too in my time to be a philosopher,' said Oliver Edwards in Boswell's *Life of Johnson*; 'but I don't know how, cheerfulness was always breaking in.' And it is this marvellous capacity for life, as the Christian knows it, to break through in the unexpected and transforming on which Auden ends the Christmas oratorio I have been quoting. It sums up also what I have been saying about the way, the truth and the life.

> He is the Way.
> Follow Him through the Land of Unlikeness;
> You will see rare beasts, and have unique
>   adventures.
>
> He is the Truth.
> Seek Him in the Kingdom of Anxiety;
> You will come to a great city that has expected
>   your return for years.
>
> He is the Life.
> Love Him in the World of the Flesh;
> And at your marriage all its occasions shall dance
>   for joy.[18]

FIVE

TOMORROW'S LAYMAN

I have tried so far to say something of the difference it makes to be a Christian today—after the end of the stable state, which settled it all for us in relatively cut-and-dried terms. I have done this under the broad headings of the way, the truth and the life. And I trust there has emerged some vision of what it means to be human now which is genuinely distinctive without being falsely distinct.

In these last two chapters I want to return to the identity crisis from which we started and ask what does acceptance of this pattern of living mean for the role of the individual Christian—or, rather, what is it going to mean in the future in contrast with the past. And one has merely to ask this question to realize its absurdity. For the end of the stable state means the end of *any* fixed pattern. Part, indeed, of the identity crisis is created precisely by the fact that the Church has hitherto imposed a singular uniformity of role —which has transcended almost every division among Christians, even so fundamental a one as that between Catholic and Protestant. For in all our traditions the meaning of being a 'good churchman' has been remarkably stereotyped, far more so than in the New Testament, where it is the differences in being a Christian that are most stressed—some apostles, some prophets, some evangelists, some pastors and teachers—a glorious welter of diversity. For if all functions were the same, where would the Body be? And the one Spirit divides not from each but to each: the differences are differences for, not differences from. And these are part of the freedom for a world whose needs are constantly diversifying. To be a Christian is to be what the French call '*disponible*', at the disposal of all, yet at the mercy of none—save one.

Yet on this moving pattern of obedience the Church has imposed its own grids or fixed orders of ministry. From time to time indeed they do get modified. There was a big shake-up at the Reformation, when the sevenfold ministry of the medieval Church was allowed to lapse into desuetude. But in its place the Reformers put (or as they thought restored) other models of ministry—threefold (as in the Anglican Church), twofold (as in the presbyterian polities), or even simple pastors (in the more evangelical sects). Significantly they all reduced rather than expanded. But above all the basic division (which owed more to the class-structure of the Roman empire than to anything in the New Testament) was retained—that between clergy and laity. In the New Testament the two words from which they come, *cleros* and *laos*, are both used to designate the whole people of God. But subsequently they are opposed, to distinguish what Gratian the medieval lawyer called the 'two sorts of Christians', not good and bad Christians, but (in army parlance) officers and men. And this line, between those above the salt and those below, became in practice more decisive (and divisive) than any differences of *office*, some of which, like deacon, were on one side of it, while others virtually indistinguishable in function, like reader, were on the other.

This has been said many times before and there is no need to expand it now. But it must be mentioned because it constitutes a major factor in the identity crisis which has overtaken both clergy and laity. Previously on this line at any rate men knew where they were (and women too—which was below it!). Now everything is in the melting, even in the Church of Rome (though we are still some distance yet from the first pope to have a husband). But rather than concentrate on this volcanic eruption within the domestic life of the Churches or speculate about the patterns of its fall-out, I want to look more fundamentally and theologically at the role of the Christian seeking responsible presence in and for tomorrow's world.

And I propose to do it under the familiar headings of 'tomorrow's layman' and 'tomorrow's priest', *not* because these are *opposed* to each other (like layman and clergyman), as I shall indeed be stressing. But, within the single vocation to be a Christian, there remain differences *for*, diversities of function and ministry. And these differences, unlike the status-marking clergy line, are native to the Church. Moreover we must start where we are. We are more likely to move to a true theology and practice by taking into account the traditional categories of layman and priest and showing how they should be related than by ignoring them.

What then is the fundamental meaning of being a layman? It has been so distorted by being defined negatively, as one who is *not* a clergyman or *not* an expert ('I'm a mere layman in this field'), that it will be good to start by saying what it is. Fundamentally, of course, it is the calling that Bonhoeffer spoke of to be a man, not a type of man—for instance, religious in a non-sacerdotal way, which is often what is meant by 'lay' spirituality—but a free, mature human being in the full stature of Jesus Christ. But if the word 'layman' is to be usefully distinguished from the word 'man', it should characterize man under certain aspects (just as to describe man as *Homo sapiens* is not to describe a type of man but man as a biological species). I would suggest two aspects that are fundamental to the notion of a layman.

(1) The first is man in his worldliness, as the Christian understands this. And it is a very distinctive kind of worldliness—what the New Testament describes as being 'in' the world but not 'of' it, or what Alec Vidler designated 'holy worldliness'. And the word 'holy' here is not intended to have some moral or religious connotation associated with 'holiness sects' or 'holier-than-thou' attitudes. It is used in the way that the Bible uses the word, to mean (as Christopher Evans, the New Testament scholar,

has put it) 'with a difference'. 'Holy Spirit' is spirit—but with a difference. When Jesus is represented as addressing God as 'holy Father' it means 'father', with all the familiar intimacy of the child's term *'abba'*, but 'with a difference'. So 'holy worldliness' is not something particularly pious but a being in the world, up to the hilt, yet with a difference. And the difference is that mysterious kind of citizenship, of belonging yet not belonging, which I tried to characterize in the second chapter on 'the way' and which is epitomized in the passage I quoted from the Epistle to Diognetus. It means being wholly involved in the world, yet not deriving one's accreditation from it; being bound to it, yet not bound by it. It is, as I said, like walking on the knife-edge of a mountain ridge, with the ever-present danger of slithering down into holy otherworldliness on the one side or into unholy worldliness on the other. And the layman is the man who walks that ridge with all the delicacy of balance and maturity of judgement which that requires.

Within this universal Christian calling there is still plenty of room for differences of vocation. To stress the 'not of' the world, which is perpetually in peril of being submerged by the 'in', the Church has always recognized the vocation of some to a relative disengagement, to a standing back *from* the world in order to be free *for* it in special ways—to be set apart, for instance, to be ministers, missionaries or monks. But two things have distorted and damaged this witness.

One is the disastrous association of having a 'vocation' with this alone—with the corollary that the majority who feel no call to this relative distancing have no vocation. Rather, such witness must be seen as the exception to the common vocation, to be a Christian (which is the only use of 'vocation' the New Testament knows) in order to prove, and improve, the rule that this calling is by definition to a worldly life.

The other distorting factor is that *all* ministers have

been assumed to have the call (to quote the Ordinal of the Church of England) 'to forsake and set aside (as much as you may) all worldly cares and studies'—just as in the Roman Catholic tradition *all* priests have been assumed to have the call to celibacy. This has meant that the word 'lay' has become associated not only with the absence of vocation but with 'worldliness' in the bad sense. '*Laïque*' in French now means 'secular' or profane in the pejorative sense of being *of* the world, worldly—in contrast to the 'religious' who are not of the world. (That this has not happened to 'lay' in English is one of the happy results of having no serious history of anti-clericalism.)

But, free of these distortions, the true vocation of the layman, the norm of being a Christian, is precisely to live with this tension, of being in the world but not of it, rather than to resolve it by separation of roles. And what this means is suggested by the illustrations Jesus himself drew from life to indicate the function of his followers in the world. They were to be like salt and leaven and light. But these are all things that are distinctively themselves only as they are immersed and apparently lost in something else. Salt kept by itself in a salt-cellar is an agglomeration of useless white crystals: it does its stuff—it preserves, heals and savours—only as it is 'in solution', dissolved and assimilated in something else. Yeast too is not only useless but actually goes off if it is kept in a jar by itself: it leavens only if, as the parable says, it is mixed and 'hidden' in a mass of dough; it changes only as it is itself changed. Light too cannot be seen for itself alone: it can only be detected by the matter it falls on and the specks it illumines.

Yet there has been a constant tendency in Christian thought and piety to suppose that the Christian is really being himself, showing his identity and difference, as he keeps himself pure and undefiled from the world, that he preserves his soul by *not* losing it. And, similarly, definitions of the Church in Christian theology have charac-

c

teristically started from the salt in the cellar, when it is 'gathered' rather than dispersed—like that of the Anglican Articles which describes it as 'a congregation of faithful men, in which the pure Word of God is preached, and the Sacraments be duly ministered'. But this 'out of the world' state, however vital to its functioning *in* the world (as breathing in is to breathing out), describes the Church precisely when it is not 'doing its own thing'. To *begin* the definition here, as though this were its normative condition, is inevitably to distort.

(2) This reference to the Church has already introduced the second aspect that marks the layman off from just any man. The first is his distinctive relationship to the world of which we have been speaking. He is as much in it as every other human being; yet he is not 'a man of the world' in the sense that *this is* his life. But, secondly, a layman, as the derivation of the word implies, is a member of the *laos*, or 'holy people'. He is called to be a person 'with a difference', which is the basic meaning of the term 'the saints' (or 'holy ones') that is so regularly in the New Testament applied to Christians. And this is something you can only be in the plural, as a member of a group. In other words, to be a layman, as we saw before, is necessarily to be in *ecclesia*, in that special relationship of corporate and conscious dedication to the kingdom of God which the Bible indicates by the people of God. To be a layman is to be a churchman,

This, of course, is so obvious and commonplace as apparently not to be worth saying. Yet I want to say it positively in order to rescue it from its negative implications. For you have only to go on to ask what it means to be a 'good churchman' to realize the appalling limitations associated with this category. It has meant being a faithful supporter of the religious organization, being everything the vicar has in mind when he speaks of 'one of my best laity' (n.b. the 'my'!).

Now the last thing I want to do is to depreciate this—

though I find it almost impossible not to *appear* to do so if one questions its limitations. The inherited structure of the Church as a religious organization is one that we dare not neglect or despise if the Church is going to be an effective instrument for anything. It does not need to be said that there are traditional congregations and parish churches which are deeply and transformingly successful —and that not merely in the superficial, worldly sense of that term.

Yet in all our traditions we stand at a critical juncture. So much of our heritage of building and organization cries out for reshaping and redeployment if the forces of renewal which are there within the Church are to be liberated for the re-creation of the world. The resources, material and human, are far too precious to waste or be left geared simply to servicing the religious club; and within the Churches there are considerable numbers who are longing for release. The transformation of the structures is something that is going to require great powers of leadership, as much from below as from above, and it is going increasingly to be a lay task. To take on the burdens and the opportunities of the institution is a responsibility (and, as I know, a reward) which someone must shoulder, and it will be tragic if all the best leadership is deployed elsewhere. Indeed it is a commitment from which no Christian can wholly opt out. In view of the virtual *equation* in many minds of laymanship with this task, it may seem ironic to have to repeat the remark of Peter Berger, the American sociologist and theologian, that 'Involvement with organized religion *is a* Christian vocation' (though only one).[1] Moreover, it is a vocation, within the manifold functions of the Church, which has acquired a disproportionate but unavoidable importance. For so largely in its history to date has Christianity been identified with what Bonhoeffer called 'a pattern of religion' that just to let this decay—literally or metaphorically to allow the church roof to fall in—would be seen by most people, inside and outside the Church, as a body-blow to the faith. The religious organization has been to most Christians what St Paul said the Mosaic law was to the Jew, 'the very shape of knowledge and truth'.[2] It has been the matrix of the way, the truth and the life. And, like the Law, in itself it is 'holy and righteous and good'. As a bishop I have been and still am very much involved with organized religion. I can testify to the potential locked up in it. But I am equally concerned to unlock it. For it is a container, I suspect, in which those of the younger generation are going to be less and less attracted to invest either their faith or their hope or their charity (all of which are considerable). To allow the role of the 'good layman' to be pictured *primarily* in terms of keeping *that* going is to invite men to look elsewhere. And that would be a tragedy.

Nevertheless, I wish to insist as strongly as ever that to-morrow's layman must be a Church-man, a man committed, with others, to the relationship of being in *ecclesia*, of conscious dedication and ministry to the things of the Kingdom. *How* he will exercise that laymanship is likely more and more to be through secular rather than religious groups. That is to say, it will be through structures, clusters, *ad hoc* and even (in the case of individual injustices) *ad hominem* associations, called forth by the requirements of *koinonia* within the world—the imperatives, and the indicatives, of freedom, justice and love—rather than through groupings which are the by-product or out-reach of the religious institution. And one of the main differences will be that these clusters will from the beginning include those who are not religious and indeed not Christian. The characteristic Church organization of the past—like, for instance, the Mothers' Union in the Church of England or the various forms of Catholic social action or Church schools or hospitals—has started from banding together Church members with a common concern for witness in the world. The characteristic grouping today consists of those called forth by a particular human need—one thinks (in Britain) of the Marriage Guidance Council, of Shelter for the homeless, of Release for drug addicts, of Oxfam, Amnesty International, and the variety of law reform and liberation movements. The composition of these will not be exclusively Christian, though their initiative and membership will often, thank God, be disproportionately Christian. The prophetic discernment that evokes them will come from involvement in the secular structures. It is these rather than religious organizations for social ends that are most likely today to be the effective channels of change—and *therefore* the place where the layman will primarily be found.

This connects with what we said earlier about *ecclesia* not being a peculiarly Christian category and about those who respond to the Kingdom without being able to name the name. For there are laymen of the latent Church too. They would not call themselves Christians, and they do not bless us for baptizing them such. Often their ends— and more frequently their means—are not identical with ours. But here above all it is the case that 'He who is not against us is for us'. And time and again in my experience there is more in common between the minorities that really share this 'lay' vocation, whatever their formulation of it, than each has with its 'own' majority.

Archbishop Helder Camara has put the matter like this:

We must try to unearth, encourage and foster the 'Abrahamic minorities' which God raises up in all countries. God loves mankind so much that he takes upon himself the task of sowing—in the most difficult environments and at the most difficult moments—'sons of Abraham', who hope against all hope, who are like small open windows that let in a little fresh air and a ray of light. To seek out these sons of hope and encourage them to promote better understanding among men and work toward building a new world—that, it seems to me, is to co-operate with the Father's plan for redeeming the world.[3]

These 'sons of Abraham' today will not be limited to Christians, just as Jesus and St Paul had to insist that they were not limited to Jews. There are many who would respond to such words who could not call themselves Christians even in the loosest and most unpackaged sense. Yet they are transformers rather than conformers. 'Adapt yourselves no longer to the pattern of this present world, but let your minds be remade and your whole nature thus transformed':[4] so said St Paul, in a truly revolutionary call. This is the vocation of the Kingdom, and humanity has desperate need of such men—whether they be in the Christian Church or not.

But they must be where the action is, and alert and sensitive to see it in time. And this may be in a cloud smaller than a man's hand. It could be that we are being called to live during this coming decade in a time of big things, but it is as likely for most of us to be a time of small things, where the discernment and the faithfulness are all. This came home to me vividly in a letter about the uphill struggle of a vicar in Aston, Birmingham merely to keep himself and his tiny fear-ful congregation a window of light in their racially twilight area. Simply to remain an open human fellowship required all the resources of the gospel.

I am not reaping the harvest [he ended]; I scarcely claim to be sowing the seed; I am hardly ploughing the soil; but I am gathering out the stones. But, unlike Robert Bruce, often my gathering out the stones causes soil erosion.

Yet the faithfulness in very small things came through the whole as a tonic of courage and hope.

'Take no thought of the harvest,' wrote T. S. Eliot, 'But only of proper sowing.'[5] And the sowing stage, Jesus knew, was concerned with the tiniest of seeds, the mere pinch of salt that makes the difference, the ounce of yeast that can lighten a mass of dough. He was not interested in a triumphalist Church standing impregnable *against* the world. He *was* interested in the force of a new life which could split rocks and move mountains. Tomorrow's layman is the person prepared—and trained—*in whatever appropriate 'ecclesial' structure* to be the channel of that force, made flesh. The structures will be of great diversity —much greater than we have hitherto allowed—from small anonymous cells to movements equipped to do battle against the principalities and powers, political and economic, of our highly collectivized national and international world.

In all this there is no room for the luxury of dissension between religious and non-religious, let alone between Christians and Christians. We are all up against it: the Victorian confidence of secularist and churchman alike has waned. 'What it takes to make and to keep life human' today is truly daunting—in face of the vampire forces of neo-colonialism sucking from the underdeveloped more than aid ever puts in, the escalating gap between rich and poor growing faster even than the population explosion, the arms race and the space drain, the mad drive for growth plundering the planet's irreplaceable resources, and the spiral of violence and the ecological Armageddon that threaten to engulf us all. As Michael Novak, the Roman Catholic layman, put it at the close of a notable article on 'The Secular Saint',

> It takes a lot of men in a lot of places to change the quality of life on this planet by so much as a featherweight. . . . We have no right to expect the world to be more than absurd. Even the sign of Jesus, the cross, is absurd. Atheist and believer share the same dark night of the soul. Let as many as can work together in that night, shaping an ecumenical movement of those who hope to diminish the number of stunted lives.[6]

On an adequate supply of such 'saints', such truly 'lay' men and women—even if no more than a remnant scattered among the nations for a witness and a sign that shall be spoken against—the hope of a new world, and perhaps of any world, in the next generation may turn.

The spiritual resources required for this secular sanctity will be as deep as ever they were, but much less narrow than our segregated spiritualities have hitherto suggested.

It is only those who achieve an inner unity within themselves and possess a worldwide vision and universal spirit who will be fit instruments to perform the miracle of combining the violence of the prophets, the truth of Christ, the revolutionary spirit of the gospel—but without destroying love.[7]

So Dom Helder Camara—himself a living disproof that being a layman in the world and an archbishop in the Church are in any sense opposed—catches both the simplicity and the complexity of such worldly holiness. It confessedly 'contradicts expectation'—but that is what 'hope against all hope' so gloriously means.

SIX

TOMORROW'S PRIEST

I began with the crisis of identity in which the contemporary Christian finds himself alike in his relation to others around him and in relation to his own past. And nowhere is this crisis focussed and intensified more than in the person of the ordained minister or priest (I shall use the latter word for shorthand purposes without ecclesiastical overtones—for at this point we are all now in the same boat). It is scarcely possible to attend a gathering of clergy without this question, spoken or unspoken, lurking somewhere in the background and scarcely a year passes without some book, or several books, appearing with titles like *Crisis in Ministry* or *Ministry in Question*. One called the latter has indeed just arrived on my desk as I write this. It is an English Free Church symposium. And its title reflects well the fundamental concern today, which is no longer simply whether the role of the priest or minister is the same (not even the Pope can think that) but whether he has any role at all. Here we really are approaching a state of 'uncertainty' in the full rigour of Donald Schon's description.

The role of the professional ministry is threatened from two sides. The pressure is partly sociological. Till now there has always been in every society and in every religion a place for the priest in the life of the village. With ever-increasing secularization that slot is threatened. Others—social workers, psychiatrists, teachers, counsellors —are taking over what he did. Is there going to be any recognizable room left for him? This is so obvious an aspect of the crisis that I need not dwell on it. But the crisis is also theological. When he alone for all practical purposes was 'in the ministry' (so that 'the ministry' *meant* 'the clergy') the distinctive function of the priest within the Body was clear. But with the rediscovery of the priesthood of the whole laity his prerogative appears to be being usurped. As the one increases, so the other, it seems, must decrease. Will there be anything that he alone can do?

The very form of the question betrays the presupposition that the difference in being a priest, like the difference in being a Christian, is primarily a difference from, and that distinctiveness consists in being distinct. For the priest has been defined in terms of what the others cannot do. There have been certain reserved functions which have been the preserve of the ordained ministry and in terms of which it has justified itself. These it has hedged around with 'the clergy line', dividing those in the 'sacred' ministry or 'holy' orders from those who are not, and it has entrenched this line with an assortment of legal, cultural and mystical sanctions. The details naturally vary with the tradition. The more Catholic its ethos, the more the magic circle is centred in the Sacraments; the more Protestant, the more it is focussed on the Word. But with the desacralization of all life the exclusive power of the priest who holds in his hands the key to the miracle evaporates except among the superstitious. With the educated society and the electronic revolution the expertise of the preacher who alone knows the answers to the ultimate questions of existence is devalued. The altar and the pulpit are no longer the self-authenticating preserves of a professional caste. Yet the threat posed by secularization, which, like socialization, is essentially a *neutral* process, *is* a-threat only because of the false criterion of 'difference' that we have watched at work all along. Let me elucidate this in relation to the two aspects of the crisis in ministry to which I referred, the sociological and the theological. And let us take the theological first, as the more fundamental.

(1) In the practice of all our traditions, priesthood or ministry has been defined and marked off as a clerisy *opposed* to a laity. But this is theologically a nonsense, as has always in theory been recognized. For clearly the priest is a part of the *laos*. Indeed, in Christianity above all, the idea of a separate priestly caste was repudiated from the beginning. In Judaism, to be sure, there was a priestly tribe set apart from the rest to do what the others could not do—and the high priest once a year to do what no one else could do. The sphere of the holy was the opposite of the common or unclean, and the relationship of the priesthood to the people was vicarious: it existed to perform holy things *instead of them*. Christianity abolished all that. The veil of the Temple was rent from top to bottom. For nearly two hundred years the words 'priest' and 'priestly' were applied solely to the Body as a whole (*presbyteros*, elder, not *hiereus*, a priest, being the term for the particular order of ministry) and 'ministry', *diaconia*, was of course a description of the activity of the whole Church prior to its technical use for the diaconate. In other words, in the great new reality of the *koinonia hagiōn* (which means not simply the communion of saints but the communalization of the holy), priesthood and ministry are there not to do what the others cannot do but to carry out *on their behalf* what all must do. The relation of those specially ordained is representative rather than vicarious.

Of course this does not preclude differentiation of function and of commissioning for particular ministries; and the New Testament clearly witnesses to this in profusion. Indeed the trouble, as I indicated earlier, is that this profusion has been disastrously restricted. Symptomatic of this is the prayer prior to the ordination of priests in the Church of England, specially written by the so-called Reformers. After listing some of the variety of Scriptural ministries—apostles, prophets, evangelists, doctors and pastors—the prayer goes on to thank God for calling the prospective priests to 'the same office and ministry'. In other words, the priesthood now includes the lot: all are swallowed up into one omnivorous order of ministry. One man is expected to do everything, the rest nothing—except, in the words of the traditional Anglican service for the induction of a new vicar, to "pray continually for this your minister who is set over you in the Lord and help him forward in all the duties of *his* holy calling'. Not only has this clericalization of the Word and Sacraments deprived and impoverished the laity (till the astonishment always to me is that there are so *many* laity in our churches not so few), but it has deterred from ordination (and rightly dissuaded the Church from ordaining) many who have *not* 'got everything'. Indeed, on this definition of the omnicompetent professional, I am convinced that we have been ordaining too many, not too few. But the Lord—and economics—is looking after that, though unfortunately the selective process is not always very sensitive: indeed, it is too often those who are most discerning that are most deterred.

But, whatever else tomorrow's priest will be, he cannot support his identity or justify his ego at the *expense* of the laity. His only role can be to serve as the *focus and intensification* of what it means to be a layman. In what sense he has a *distinctive* vocation I shall be coming to later. But first let me stress his solidarity too with regard to the other mark we noted of the layman—not only full membership of the *laos*, but a very characteristic and distinctive *worldliness*.

Traditionally—though it was not so from the beginning —the calling to be a priest or minister has, as we saw, been equated with forsaking worldly cares and studies (and none were keener on this than the Reformers, in reaction against the unholy worldliness of the medieval clerisy). It has been one of the marks of difference from the laity that, relatively speaking, the priest has *not* been in the world, earning his own living. Originally this grew

up for purely functional reasons, of freedom *for*, release
to do the work of an apostle or evangelist or teacher.
And St Paul recognizes—and indeed insists on—complete
personal liberty in this matter: it is purely a question of
vocation and circumstance. But it was not long before it
became an issue of freedom *from* the world and came to
be imposed on all (or most) clergy. And this is still the
norm.

In that English Free Church symposium I mentioned,
Caryl Micklem quotes the latest regulations for the Con-
gregational ministry (ostensibly the 'freest' and least struc-
tured of all), which were redrafted *in 1970* to state: 'A
candidate shall be expected to offer himself for full-time
service in the Ministry'. 'Note,' he comments, 'the tell-tale
capital,' and he adds:

> This provision, which appears in writing for the first
> time now, means in effect that a man or a woman [and
> at least the Congregationalists have *that* freedom!] will
> not be accepted for theological training and commis-
> sioned service among our churches unless ready and
> able to cast his or her vocation in the mould of being 'a
> minister' in charge of 'a local church'. My guess is that
> the numbers of those so willing and able will dwindle
> almost to nothing during the next few years (they are
> already down to a trickle); while the numbers of those
> willing to undergo training in order to make themselves
> theologically literate and then work in, and round the
> edges of, local and professional and occupational church
> groups on a voluntary and part-time basis will increase.[1]

For himself, he confesses, after twenty fulfilled years as
a full-time minister, that if he were asked today, 'Do you
offer yourself for full-time service in the Ministry?', he
would have to reply:

> Because I am not a scholar, or administrator, or crowd-
> person [that is, in his useful distinction, one called to
> minister to men in the mass, as opposed to small groups]
> I cannot say so. And I doubt if the day after tomorrow

I shall even know, except in memory, what you mean.[2] That is doubtless an exaggeration, though I should be prepared to guess that in twenty-five years from now in my own Church priests in secular jobs (at present still a tiny minority) will outnumber those who are not. And this will be (I hope) not merely for economic reasons but because of that very freedom *for* the world which in other circumstances made men give up secular work—and which will make many still. For above all the Church must be free in this regard, to call men in and out of its full-time employment—as it does the non-ordained. And among the conditions of this freedom are that it must not ordain men who have not got a secular qualification and that it must not imply any undertaking that ordination automatically carries with it a guaranteed income to retirement and beyond.

(2) This has already involved us in the second, sociological, pressure, which is threatening to erode 'the Ministry' as a separate career. Its distinctiveness has hitherto been assured by its being *a* profession amongst others, with its own carefully controlled entry, standards of training, professional code and career-structure (all laid down from the centre, which has successfully created, in Ivan Illich's phrase, 'a captive profession out of a free vocation'[3]). And until the day before yesterday the priest-hood had its clearly recognized place in society, along-side doctors, lawyers and the rest. There are countries no doubt where this stable state still obtains. Certainly in Britain it is not ill will or anti-clericalism that is squeez-ing it out as a profession. It is simply that what activity is left to its specialist expertise comes increasingly to feel like minding a pool out of the main stream of life. As Alistair Kee has put it with pardonable sharpness, instead of being 'one of the most dynamic, exciting, rewarding and creative careers in a modern society', 'ordination is a passport to limbo'.[4] The 'cure' or care for which tradition-ally the parson has stood is being taken over by those with

more specialist disciplines. If he is to compete, he has to acquire one of these—or tag along as an amateur.

This again is a very familiar observation. But let me use it as a way into what I believe may be the clue to the genuine distinctiveness of the priest. The priesthood has been *a* profession. That is an historically conditioned phenomenon. But, in the root sense of the word, the priest is properly and essentially a pro-fessional person. That is to say, he is there to 'speak for' others. The word comes from the same source as 'prophet' (and indeed 'professor'—though it is significant how ironic this seems: in the popular mind the professor is more remote and cut off than the parson!). As a professional, the priest is a man for others—speaking for them, acting for them, suffering for them. For that at their best is what the professions in society exist to do—like the doctor or the social worker or the advocate. Such men are not merely in it, as we say, for themselves, but for others.

In this of course the priest is not *contrasted* with other Christians. All laity are called to follow the man for others. But there is a true sense in which the priest is called to be that to them, to be, like the Pope, 'the servant of the servants of God'. This again is a focussing and intensification of the role of the laity, not a difference from it: it is taking further the principle of the *pars pro toto*, the part for the whole. And an essential element in ordination (often obscured in our practice) is that the candidate is proposed and put forward by the congregation from which he comes and commissioned to be there.

And 'there' is also *'pro'* in the other sense of that prefix —out in front, exposed. For being a prophet, being a spokesman, involves that. In bitter irony St Paul writes that being an apostle feels like being put forward as an exhibit in the world's arena—a fool for Christ's sake, a fall-guy for the kingdom of heaven. Peter Berger has written of the minister's role as a clown, and Harvey Cox of Christ's as a harlequin. In more down-to-earth terms,

Michael Wilson, an English doctor-priest, speaks of the role of a chaplain to those in hospital:

> He will take his place with many others who serve them, to serve them in the distinctive way of an openly identified man of God. Indeed perhaps the greatest tension a priest must bear is the fact that he openly stands for a God of love in a place of suffering.[5]

This perhaps begins to catch the distinctiveness of the priest. It is certainly not a distinctiveness of separation (it will be with 'many others who serve', both in the Church and in the world) and it is certainly not because he is 'a man of God' whereas others (again both in the Church and the world) are not. But he *is* a man marked out, openly identified. This will increasingly not be by the peculiar clothes or the detached parsonage by which he has hitherto been recognized. Indeed, it is likely to be by nothing that takes him *out* of the lump. He will share to the full the paradoxical character of the Christian way: 'As God's servants,' says St Paul again, 'we are the unknown men whom all men know.'[6] Yet he will, by calling and training, have the distinctive role in the dispensation of the Spirit of being the resource man for others— and that by being the back-room boy as much as by any pre-eminence.

How will he do this? The answers imply a revaluation not a devaluation of the traditional categories. The characteristic way in which a priest acts for others is as a breaker and sharer of bread, as a focus of community and communion in the broadest sense. And in the future this ministry is likely more and more to be exercised outside any consecrated building or special robes. He will take and break and make the bread of life where he is. But, equally, he is a breaker and communicator of the Word— not primarily in the sense of standing up and preaching sermons in church, but in the sense of enabling the truth of God (and of man) to break out of and into the life-situations and conversations of 'his' world ('Sermon' comes

after all from the Latin word for conversation, not mono-
logue). Again, he is the man for others in the sense that
he is specially trained and commissioned to be available
to men, at their points of strength and weakness, to help
them to become free (this is what 'absolution' means). A
parson is not someone who is parsonic but a true person,
who can liberate others to be persons.

Michael Wilson summarizes the matter thus, writing of
the hospital chaplain but in words that have a much wider
reference:

> He is one of the most public of men, yet his basic
> work is done in privacy as well as community: he is a
> man of God, with God and for God, which marks him
> out as intensely human, able to quicken the humanity
> of others. Marcel wrote: 'A really alive person is not
> merely someone who has a taste for life, but someone
> who spreads that taste, showering it, as it were, around
> him; and a person who is really alive in this way has,
> quite apart from any tangible achievements of his, some-
> thing essentially creative about him.' Of Charles de
> Foucauld it was said: 'His vocation was one of being
> present among people.'[7]

Of course a man or woman does not *have* to be ordained
to be this—that is precisely the point I was making
before about the priest not being distinguished by what
the others cannot do. And, God knows, there are priests,
'pro-men', of the latent Church too—yes, we can gladly
say there are more of them than in the religious organization. If St Paul can speak, as he does in Romans 13, of the
government authorities of a pagan empire as *leitourgoi
theou*, liturgists in divine service, we can surely recognize
priestly functions in the fields of community development,
communication, and counselling. What ordination gives is
the 'open identification'—what I spoke of earlier as the
'naming' or recognition. And this, as with the presence
of God or the anonymous Christian, is often a matter of
spotting the incognito after the event—acknowledging *de*

jure what is true *de facto*, as St Peter did in the case of Cornelius in Acts 10. And the response is: 'What prevents?' Why should the Church *not* lay hands on those whom the Spirit has already marked out as the effective men and women for others in their own communities? The call to ordination is, I suggest, increasingly going to come this way, not from on high by some unmediated vocation from above (which is then channelled down from the centre to the periphery), but out of the midst, thrown up by the local group (with such wider acknowledgement, training and authorization as is needed).

It will not require the kind of person who 'has everything' in order, as at present, to be licensed for everything. It need not be for life in the sense of duration, though it will unreservedly be for life in the sense of direction. Nor will it necessarily be full-time in economic terms, though being a priest, like being a layman or being a man, is essentially a full-time vocation. What is purchased by setting free from other employment is time—time for persons; and there is no necessary virtue in boasting with St Paul that 'we wear ourselves out working with our own hands'.[8] But equally we may buy time at the cost of place —the capacity to minister to people where they are because we are there too, 'sitting where they sit', not necessarily geographically but exposed to the same pressures and insecurities. The freedom *from* can destroy the freedom *for*, as the Churches—like the trade unions and the politicians—have found. But there is room for every sort of ministry, and the more variety and equality and cross-fertilization between them the healthier.

For the Church of the future must not be bound to any 'one-type soldier army' (as Bishop Emmerich of Michigan has described its conventional ministry) nor tied to any uniform hierarchical structure. This does not of course mean (despite the reaction I meet to such statements) that it should have *no* structure. Anyone committed to a revolution (and the Church is committed to nothing less) who said it needed no organization could scarcely expect to be taken seriously. On the contrary, the service of the Kingdom demands of the Church the most disciplined and flexible deployment of its resources. Above all it requires of it the freedom, like the press or a relief organization, to be *responsive*, in terms of money and man-power and imagination, to where the needs and the initiatives are, and to back experiments, particularly on the frontiers of social change, *whether or not they are started by Christians*. The World Council of Churches, despite its top-level status, is often showing the way here to the slower moving denominational hierarchies encumbered with their weight of immovable plant and non-terminable appointments.

Traditionally, ordination, the Church's seal of accreditation, has been restricted to two forms of ministry only—of Word and Sacrament—and they have been frozen into indelible 'orders'. But apostolicity—which simply means being sent—is after all just a way of designating 'our man in——'. And the functions acknowledged can be as varied and as variable as the Spirit requires. We are moving, as Alvin Toffler insists in his *Future Shock*, not towards the super-organization, but 'beyond bureaucracy' and the 'collapse of hierarchy' to 'the new ad-hocracy'.[9] Yet in an increasingly diversified world, the Christian Church will surely be failing humanity if, *in addition* to encouraging specialized ministries, it cannot as in the past free men simply to be men—present among people, available as whole-makers.

For we should not allow ourselves to be intimidated either by the theological or by the sociological pressures on the role of the priest—any more than by the squeezing out of 'the God of the gaps'. For 'take-over' by the laity or other professions is a threat only on a false theology of difference. The priest of the gaps, the minister of 'religion', is not the authentic Christian concept of 'the man of God'. This, rather, is the person, *whatever* his specific function in Church or world, who is called to be the whole man, in the midst, for others. Like his master, the complete layman as well as 'the high priest of our profession', who yet occupied no niche secular or ecclesiastical, he is there, ultimately, himself to *be* the place of at-one-ment. To serve as this for alienated humanity he may be forced outside the camp—any camp—on to the cross. And this after all is the only *distinctive* place which the New Testament holds out for the Christian. The anxiety to find another, some less vulnerable *locus standi*, is a false anxiety. And this and no other is also the place of resurrection and of life.

'Therefore,' says St Paul, after expatiating (in 2 Corinthians 4 and 5) as no Church bureaucrat would dare on the forces of decay and death that constantly erode the Christian ministry, 'we never cease to be confident.' The difference in being a Christian today is, I believe, exciting rather than bewildering. Or rather, it is exciting *as* it is bewildering. The search for identity (which, truly considered, is not a threat but a pilgrimage) is in depth an exploration into God. The crisis, as the word implies, is a creative act of judgement, however painful. And I for one —for all my rootage in the past, for which I am constantly grateful—do not bewail the end of the stable state. Many things must be shaken in our day if the Kingdom which cannot be shaken is to be discerned and exposed.

NOTES

Chapter 1

1. Donald Schon, 'Change and Industrial Society', *Listener*, 19 Nov. 1970, p. 686. In the subsequent book of the lectures, *Beyond the Stable State* (Maurice Temple-Smith, London, 1971), this engaging imagery has unfortunately disappeared.
2. Peter Lewis, 'The Pope and the Archbishop', *Daily Mail*, 5 Dec. 1970.
3. The programme was prepared by Ivor Smith-Cameron, Chaplain to the West London Colleges.
4. Dietrich Bonhoeffer, *Letters and Papers from Prison*, 3rd edition (SCM Press, London, 1967), p. 198.
5. Luke 21:25–28.
6. F. J. A. Hort, *The Way, the Truth, the Life* (Macmillan, London, 1893), pp. 86, 89.
7. Thomas Kretz, 'Old Tom's Scruples', *Christian Century*, 12 Nov. 1969, p. 1449. Italics mine.
8. Acts 6:13–14.
9. John 2:19.

Chapter 2

1. W. H. Auden, *For the Time Being* (Faber & Faber, London, 1945), pp. 85–86.
2. *The Way, the Truth, the Life*, pp. 55–56.
3. Romans 12:17; 1 Peter 2:12.
4. Luke 6:32–36.
5. Matthew 5:48.
6. Paul Gerhardt, 'The duteous day now closeth', verse 2, lines 5–6.
7. *For the Time Being*, p. 104.
8. The Epistle to Diognetus, Chaps 5 and 6; tr. J. B. Lightfoot, *The Apostolic Fathers* (Macmillan, London, 1893), pp. 505–507.
9. 2 Corinthians 6:8–10.
10. David Riesman, *The Lonely Crowd* (Yale University Press, 1950), Chaps. 6 and 7.
11. Rubem A. Alves, *A Theology of Human Hope* (Corpus Books, Washington, D.C., 1969), p. 155.

Chapter 3

1. Dorothee Sölle, 'Why does Theology Change?', *The Truth Is Concrete* (tr. D. Livingstone, Burns & Oates, London, 1969), Chap. 3.
2. Paul Ferris, *The Church of England* (Gollancz, London, 1962), p. 219.
3. H. A. Williams, *The True Wilderness* (Constable, London, 1965), p. 8.
4. Alec Vidler, BBC Television, 4 November 1962.
5. John Henry Newman, 'Firmly I believe and truly', lines 1–4.
6. Geoffrey Chapman, London, 1966 and 1967.
7. Langdon Gilkey, *Naming the Whirlwind* (Bobbs Merrill, Indianapolis, 1969), p. 364.
8. Cf. Mark 9:37.
9. Jeremiah 22:15–16.
10. John 3:21; 7:17.
11. Acts 17:23.
12. Cornelius A. van Peursen, 'Him Again', *Risk* (World Council of Churches, Geneva), III 4, 1967.
13. Exodus 3:14.
14. Peter Lewis, op. cit.
15. 1 John 5:20.
16. Alistair Kee, *The Way of Transcendence* (Penguin, Harmondsworth, 1971), p. 193.
17. Ibid., Chap. 6.

Chapter 4

1. John 20:31.
2. John 6:51.
3. John 1:4, 9.
4. Philippians 1:21.
5. *Letters and Papers from Prison*, p. 198.
6. Dag Hammarskjöld, *Markings* (Faber & Faber, London, 1964), p. 108.
7. 1 John 3:14.
8. Monica Furlong, *Travelling In* (Hodder & Stoughton, London, 1971), pp. 74–75.
9. Paraphrased from an address at the requiem for Fr Geoffrey Beaumont, *Quarterly Review of the Community of the Resurrection* (Mirfield, Michaelmas 1970), no. 270, p. 4.
10. 2 Corinthians 5:14.
11. Collins, London, 1969.
12. *Letters and Papers from Prison*, p. 209.
13. Op. cit., *Listener*, 10 Dec. 1970, p. 812.

14. Cf. my earlier books, *The New Reformation?* and *Christian Freedom in a Permissive Society* (SCM Press, London, 1965 and 1970).
15. John 6:35, 51.
16. Fred Brown, *Faith without Religion* (SCM Press, London, 1971) p. 149.
17. Sydney Carter, 'Lord of the Dance', *Songs of Sydney Carter: In the Present Tense*, Bk. 2 (Galliard, Great Yarmouth, 1969), pp. 4–5.
18. *For the Time Being*, p. 124.

Chapter 5

1. Peter Berger, *The Noise of Solemn Assemblies* (Doubleday, New York, 1961), p. 174. Italics mine.
2. Romans 2:20.
3. Helder Camara, 'Dichotomy Then Integration', *New Christian*, 14 May 1970, p. 6.
4. Romans 12:2.
5. T. S. Eliot, 'The Rock', *Collected Poems 1909–1935* (Faber & Faber, London, 1936), p. 159.
6. Michael Novak, 'The Secular Saint', *The Center Magazine* (Center for the Study of Democratic Institutions, Santa Barbara, California), I 4 (May 1968), p. 59.
7. *Church and Colonialism* (Sheed & Ward, London, 1969), p. 111.

Chapter 6

1. Caryl Micklem, *Ministry in Question*, ed. A. Gilmore (Darton, Longman & Todd, London, 1971), p. 26.
2. Ibid., pp. 26–27.
3. In an unpublished collection of articles, *The Breakdown of Schools* (Centro Intercultural de Documentation, Cuernavaca, Mexico, 1971).
4. *The Way of Transcendence*, p. 145.
5. Michael Wilson, *The Hospital—A Place of Truth* (Institute for the Study of Worship and Religious Architecture, University of Birmingham, 1971), p. 104.
6. 2 Corinthians 6:4, 9.
7. Op. cit., p. 105.
8. 1 Corinthians 4:12.
9. Alvin Toffler, *Future Shock* (Bodley Head, London, 1970). Chap. 7.

INDEX